C000319153

ESSENTI

BUDAPEST

Original text by Rob Stuart

Updated by Neal Bedford

© Automobile Association Developments Limited 2008

First published 2008

ISBN: 978-0-7495-5101-8

Published by AA Publishing, a trading name of Automobile Association Developments Limited, whose registered office is Fanum House, Basing View, Basingstoke, Hampshire RG21 4EA.

Registered number 1878835.

Colour separation: MRM Graphics Ltd

Printed and bound in Italy by Printer Trento S.r.l.

A03164

Maps in this title produced from:

mapping © MAIRDUMONT / Falk Verlag 2007

mapping © ISTITUTO GEOGRAFICO DE AGOSTINI S.p.A., NOVARA 2006

Transport map © Communicarta Ltd, UK

About this book

This book is divided into six sections:

The essence of Budapest pages 6–19
Introduction; Features; Food and drink;
Short break

Planning pages 20–33
Before you go; Getting there; Getting
around; Being there

Best places to see pages 34–55
The unmissable highlights of any visit
to Budapest

Best things to do pages 56–71
Great cafés; stunning views; places to
take the children and more

Exploring pages 72–169
The best places to visit in Budapest,
organized by area

Excursions pages 170–183
Places to visit out of town

Maps

All map references are to the maps on
the covers. For example, Országház has
the reference ➕ 3F – indicating the grid
square in which it is to be found

Admission Prices

Inexpensive (under 600Ft)
Moderate (600Ft–1,200Ft)
Expensive (over 1,200Ft)

Hotel prices

Prices for an ensuite double room with
breakfast in high season:
€ inexpensive (under 25,000Ft)
€€ moderate (25,000–45,000Ft)
€€€ expensive (over 45,000Ft)

Restaurant prices

Price per person, without drinks:
€ inexpensive (under 2,500Ft)
€€ moderate (2,500–5,500Ft)
€€€ expensive (over 5,500Ft)

Contents

The essence of...

Straddling the Danube with its nine bridges, Budapest has a bewildering array of architectural styles, a legacy of its turbulent history. Art nouveau, neoclassical, neo-Gothic, neo-Renaissance are just a few, and help create a skyline of astonishing grandeur. Budapest is not just a capital city, it is also a city of empire. Its sobriquet 'Queen of the Danube' is rightly deserved. But make no mistake – far from being regally remote and austere, this queen dresses rather elegantly, is modishly cosmopolitan and is inclined to drive in the fast lane.

THE ESSENCE OF BUDAPEST

features

If Europe has a centre, then it is Budapest. Hungary's capital not only straddles the Danube with ease and grace, but also the Continent's east-west divide. Here the two faces of Europe mingle, sometimes in harmony, at other times with unwanted friction. It is a place where the morning can be spent in the splendour of a royal palace and the afternoon hunting through a flea market for Russian cameras and GDR memorabilia. Or the entire day can be devoted to shopping for clothes, gorgeous antiques and authentic folk art. It doesn't really matter what you do, there's no escaping Budapest's unique charm.

It's no big surprise Budapest has a case of split personality though. On the west bank of the Danube is hilly Buda, the medieval heart of the city and favourite of the upper classes, and on the east is flat Pest (pronounced 'pesht'), the commercial centre where the buzz of city life is loudest. But considering its history, it should be psychotic. Ruled by the Turks for 150 years, dominated by the Habsburgs for generations, scarred by two world wars, shrouded by the Soviet Iron Curtain for decades, and swamped by western consumerism in the last 15 years, Budapest has at times suffered terribly. Yet it has come through it all largely intact and with tremendous energy.

Even on a short visit, it's impossible not to be

swept along by the city's vibrancy. And there is one thing Budapest will always provide: experiences. Mostly good, sometimes bad, but they will certainly always be memorable.

GEOGRAPHY

Hungary occupies the Carpathian Basin, a vast plain at the heart of East Central Europe. The River Danube divides Hungary's 93,030sq km (35,900sq miles) into the Great Plain (the Nagyalföld) on the east and Transdanubia (Dunántúl) on the west. The Great Plain is reminiscent of the Ukrainian steppes and the American prairie. Hungary's 'mountains' are little more than hills, seldom exceeding 1,000m (3,280ft) in height. The highest peak is Kékes (1,014m/ 3,326ft) in the Mátra range northeast of Budapest. Much of Hungary is less than 200m (656ft) above sea level. Lake Balaton, southwest of Budapest, is the largest freshwater lake in Europe.

ECONOMY

Budapest is the commercial and industrial heart of Hungary. A burgeoning service sector, partly the result of booming tourism, is a major employer, though traditional manufacturing industries such as textiles, chemicals, iron and steel also employ a significant part of the population. With the advent

of the free-market economy, Hungary has attracted substantial foreign investment, noticeably in the sectors of car assembly, high-tech electronics and light manufacturing.

LANGUAGE

Hungarian is a difficult language at which a guess can lead to real confusion. German, which up until now has been the second language, is now being overtaken by English, especially among the young.

food & drink

Ask anyone to name a Hungarian dish and the answer invariably will be goulash. They will also make the mistake of calling it a 'stew' when it is in fact a soup. Perhaps because of decades of Communism, Central European cuisine has been associated with the sort of meal one would describe politely as filling, nutritious, yet unimaginative – a misconception. Although Hungarian cooking may struggle to compete with Europe's finest cuisine, its heartiness and unmistakable paprika flavours are enjoyed with gusto by anyone who has the privilege to sample it.

CHARACTERISTIC FEATURES OF HUNGARIAN COOKING

Traditional Hungarian 'peasant' cooking is based on

the use of *rantas*, a rich roux of flour and pork lard. Bland and heavy, it requires lashings of paprika to spice it up. Paprika is still widely used and now thought of as a defining feature of Hungarian cooking. As the saying goes, 'a real Magyar can handle his strong paprika well'. Another characteristic is the use of sour cream, which adds a

sharpness to the flavour. Soups and pasta also figure strongly, with the ever-present paprika either on the table or already in the dish. However, Hungarian cuisine prides itself on being rich, full of flavour, and substantial.

THE CARNIVORE AND THE VEGETARIAN

Most, if not all, Hungarian menus are dominated by meat dishes. Favourite meats are chicken (their livers are a Hungarian speciality), pork, veal, venison, duck and beef. Sometimes you can discover, as with 'Tenderloin Steak Budapest Style', for instance, any number of different meats mixed together. In this case, the steak sits alongside smoked bacon, pork bones and goose livers. Hence Hungarian cuisine's reputation for richness. Fish is also well represented on Hungarian menus, especially pike, carp, perch and trout.

As a landlocked country, the scarcity of sea fish is not surprising, but if anyone can turn a pike or carp (fish generally frowned upon elsewhere) into a mouth-watering dish, it's the Hungarians. Pike dumplings are delicious in a dill sauce, as is carp served with mushrooms in a sour cream sauce. Vegetarians shouldn't entirely despair. Most restaurants, even those with busy staff, will be sympathetic to dietary preferences and palates.

WINES, BEERS AND SPIRITS

We are all familiar with Hungarian Merlot and Cabernet Sauvignon reds and whites, also with the legendary Egri Bikaver (Bull's Blood) which once rubbed corks on the lower shelves with popular *vins de table*. This wine is still very popular in Hungary, but for superior quality try Vesztzergombi Bikavér from the Szekeszárd region. Other good, often rather heavy reds come from the vineyards in the Villány area to the southeast of Pécs. White wines of quality are produced on the shores of Lake Balaton, the most interesting ones coming from the small vineyards in the lovely hilly country rising from the north shore. Tokaji is what Louis XIV of France called 'the wine of kings, the king of wines'. Rumour has it that since so little of this exceptional white wine is produced from that region, you're bound to buy a fake bottle. This is not quite true.

The best Hungarian beers are Kőbányai and Dreher, but you'll also find an abundance of familiar foreign brands. Traditional Hungarian spirits are brandies called *pálinka*, and are available in various flavours such as cherry, plum and ,most famously, apricot (*barackpálinka*). Be warned though: they are generally strong. Otherwise, all the usual spirits are available, for example whisky, vodka and gin. Those who prefer soft drinks can get anything from mineral water to cola.

short break

If you only have a short time to visit Budapest, or would like to get a really complete picture of the city, here are the essentials:

● **Muse on, or be amused by,** Halászbástya (Fishermen's Bastion), an architectural fantasy that wouldn't look out of place on a Disney set (➤ 40–41).

● **Visit Vörösmarty tér**, a pedestrianized and peaceful square, but only after you've browsed the most exclusive shopping street, Váci utca (➤ 119).

● **Stand atop Gellért-hegy** (Gellért Hill) for spectacular views of the city, as well as the Citadella, a fortress built of white stone (➤ 38–39).

● **Marvel at the architectural** magnificence of Országház, the Parliament building (➤ 48–49).

● **Wander the picturesque streets** of Vár-hegy (Castle Hill), or just soak up the atmosphere at one of the many bars and cafés there (➤ 54–55).

● **Take a relaxing dip** in one of the many *gyógyfürdő* (thermal baths) if foot-sore from trudging the streets.

● **Stroll down Andrássy út,** once the most fashionable place to promenade in Budapest (➤ 138).

● **Take refuge from the hustle of the city** on peaceful Margit-sziget (Margaret Island) in the middle of the Danube (➤ 44–45).

● **Visit the Budai Királyi Palota** (Buda Royal Palace) and the several museums in its confines (➤ 36–37).

● **Admire Mátyás-templom** (Matthias Church) in all its neo-Gothic magnificence in Trinity Square (➤ 46–47).

Planning

Before you go

WHEN TO GO

JAN	FEB	MAR	APR	MAY	JUN	JUL	AUG	SEP	OCT	NOV	DEC
0°C	0°C	10°C	18°C	22°C	25°C	28°C	26°C	24°C	16°C	8°C	0°C
32°F	32°F	50°F	64°F	72°F	79°F	82°F	79°F	75°F	61°F	46°F	32°F

⬤ High season ⬤ Low season

Temperatures are the average daily maximum for each month. Budapest is located in a temperate zone, and has a Continental climate characterized by cold winters (average temperature -2°C/28°F), hot summers (average temperature 22°C/71°F), and a fair amount of rain in spring and autumn. Weather-wise, the best months to visit are May, June, September and October when temperatures are moderate, and clear, blue skies feature regularly as a city backdrop. That's not to say Budapest isn't gorgeous under a blanket of winter snow, just remember to bring a very warm coat. July and August can bring uncomfortably high temperatures.

Festivals are held throughout the year, but the largest concentration occur in spring and autumn (➤ 24–25).

WHAT YOU NEED

		UK	Germany	USA	Netherlands	Spain
●	Required					
○	Suggested					
▲	Not required	Some countries require a passport to remain valid for a minimum period (usually at least six months) beyond the date of entry – contact their consulate or embassy or your travel agent for details.				
Passport or National Identity Card where applicable		●	●	●	●	●
Visa (regulations can change, check before your journey)		▲	▲	▲	▲	▲
Onward or Return Ticket		▲	▲	▲	▲	▲
Health Inoculations		▲	▲	▲	▲	▲
Health Documentation (➤ 23, Health Insurance)		●	●	○	○	●
Travel Insurance		○	○	○	○	○
Driving Licence (National or International)		●	●	●	●	●
Car Insurance Certificate (if own car)		●	●	●	●	●
Car registration document (if own car)		●	●	●	●	●

WEBSITES

- National Tourist Information Centre: www.tourinform.hu
- Budapest Tourist Office: www.budapestinfo.hu
- Hungarian Arts Festivals Federation: www.artsfestivals.hu
- Budapest Week: www.budapestweek.com

TOURIST OFFICES AT HOME

In the UK

Hungarian National Tourist Board
46 Eaton Place
London SW1X 8AL
☎ 020 7823 1032;
www.gotohungary.co.uk

In the USA

Hungarian Tourism Board
350 Fifth Avenue, Suite 7107
New York NY 10118
☎ 212/695 1221;
www.gotohungary.com

In Canada

Embassy of the Republic of Hungary
302 Metcalfe Street
Ottawa, Ontario K2P 1S2
☎ (613) 230-2717

In Australia

Consulate General of Hungary
Suite 405, 203–233 New South Head Road, Edgecliff, NSW 2027
☎ (02) 9328 7859;
www.hunconsydney.com

HEALTH INSURANCE

All visitors to Hungary receive free first aid and transport to hospital. Although citizens of EU countries are entitled to free further treatment, comprehensive health insurance is recommended. Non-EU citizens should make sure they have full health cover.

TIME DIFFERENCES

GMT	Budapest	Germany	USA (NY)	Netherlands	Spain
12 noon	1PM	1PM	7AM	1PM	1PM

Hungary is on Central European Time, one hour ahead of Greenwich Mean Time (GMT+1), but from early March to late October, daylight saving (GMT+2) operates.

NATIONAL HOLIDAYS

1 Jan *New Year's Day*

15 Mar *Anniversary of 1848–9 Revolution*

Mar/Apr *Easter Monday*

1 May *Labour Day*

May/Jun *Whit Monday*

20 Aug *St Stephen's Day*

23 Oct *Anniversary of 1956 Revolution*

1 Nov *All Saints' Day*

25 Dec *Christmas Day*

26 Dec *Boxing Day*

In Hungary most offices, shops and other facilities close down on public holidays and, should any of these holidays be on a Tuesday or Thursday, the day between it and the weekend also becomes a public holiday.

WHAT'S ON WHEN

March *Budapest Spring Festival:* First-class concerts, opera, dance, theatre and folklore performances as well as master classes and exhibitions at several venues in the city.

April *National Dance House Meeting and Fair,* Budapest Sports Arena: A whirl of music and dance lessons, amateur and professional performances, folk artists and handicraft displays.

June *Week of Books:* A celebration of Hungarian literature, with interviews, performances and publishing-house stalls around the city centre.

Wine Festival, Városliget: A gastronomic festival in the City Park featuring top wines and winemakers, gypsy and folk music, and a lively market atmosphere.

Bridge Festival: A carnival marks the anniversary of the Széchenyi Lánchíd (Chain Bridge) with festivities taking on and around the bridge.

Budapest Fair, Hősök tere: This summer carnival commemorates the withdrawal of Soviet troops from Hungary. Features Jazz and classical music, street theatre and children's entertainment.

July *Summer on the Chain Bridge:* Each weekend in July, the city's oldest bridge is taken over by pedestrians, with free music concerts, performances, entertainment taking place.

Budafest Summer Music Festival: Opera, ballet and jazz in the Hilton Hotel's Dominican Courtyard, symphony orchestras outside St Stephen's Basilica, and opera and ballet at the Opera House (➤ 42).

August *Sziget Festival:* A week-long Hungarian 'Woodstock', with top international bands attracting around 400,000 visitors to Óbuda Island.

St Stephen's Day: Countrywide celebrations, processions and fireworks.

Budapest Parade: Carnival floats parade along Andrássy út, with parties starting up in the Stadium Gardens after 10pm.

Jewish Summer Festival, Jewish district: a week celebrating Jewish culture, with books, films, gastronomy, music and dance in the Jewish district (late August – early September).

September *Budafok Wine Festival,* Budafok Cellars: Cellar tours, wine-tasting, concerts, music and dance.

International Wine Fair, Buda Royal Palace: Cultural programme and grape-harvest procession.

SzeptemberFeszt: A three-day gastronomic festival with various cooking competitions, music and children's entertainment.

October *Budapest Autumn Festival:* A contemporary arts festival focusing on new directions on in music, theatre, dance, fine art, film and literature.

December *Budapest Christmas,* Vörösmarty ter: Arts and crafts sold in the city centre alongside steaming vats of mulled wine.

New Year's Eve Gala and Ball, Opera House: A gala concert in the beautiful Opera House, with a festive supper prepared by chefs from Gundel restaurant, followed by a New Year's Ball until dawn.

Getting there

BY AIR

Budapest, Ferihegy Airport,

20/24km (12/15 miles) to city centre

🚋 N/A

🚌 Minibus 1 hour

🚗 30 minutes

Keleti, Nyugati and Déli Stations

1.5km (0.93 miles) to city centre

🚋 Few stops on metro

🚌 Rail bus service

🚗 N/A

Budapest's Ferihegy Airport (☎ 296 7000, www.bud.hu) receives flights from across the globe, although the majority arrive from the continent via Europe's major airlines. Hungary's national airline, Malév (☎ in Hungary 06 40 212 121, www.malev.hu), has direct flights to/from North America and much of Europe, including the UK and Ireland. Air Berlin (www.airberlin.com), EasyJet (www.easyjet.com), SkyEurope (www.skyeurope.com) and Wizzair (www.wizzair.com) all connect Budapest with many European cities at budget prices.

BY RAIL

Budapest is linked to Europe's comprehensive rail network by Magyar Államvasutak (www.mav.hu), Hungary's state railways. International trains call at one of the city's three main stations:
Keleti (east) ✉ Kerepesi út 2–6, Budapest VII ☎ 313 6835;
Déli (south) ✉ Krisztina körút 37, Budapest I ☎ 375 6897;
Nyugati (west) ✉ Teréz körút 55–57, Budapest VI ☎ 349 0115.

BY CAR

The M1 links Budapest with Vienna, the M7 heads southwest to Croatia via Lake Balaton, the M5 travels south towards Serbia, and the M3 leads east as far as the city of Nyíregyháza.

BY BUS

Eurolines (www.eurolines.com) buses travel from London and many points on the Continent to Budapest, arriving at Népliget bus station (✉ Üllði út 131, Budapest IX ☎ 219 8000) in Pest.

BY BOAT

Ferries and hydrofoils travel between Vienna and Budapest on the Danube from April to October. They dock at the Nemzetközi hajóállomás (International Ferry Pier, Belgrád rakpart, Budapest V), located in Pest between the Erzsébet híd and Szabadság híd.

For more information see www.mahartpassnave.hu or www.ddsg-blue-danube.at.

Getting around

PUBLIC TRANSPORT

Metro As well as the below-street and rather charming M1 or *földalatti* ('underground') which has linked central Pest with Heroes' Square since 1896, there are two deep Metro lines M2 (red) and M3 (blue) connecting the city centre with the main railway stations and some of the suburbs.

Buses Around 200 trolleybus routes fill in the gaps between the tram and the Metro network. One of the easiest ways of getting up Castle Hill is to take the dinky Várbusz (castle bus) from Moskva tér.

River boats The scheduled passenger service operating on the Danube (May–Aug Thu–Sun 9–5) is an excellent and inexpensive way of seeing the city from a fresh angle.

Trams These connect many important tourist destinations and can be an excellent way of sightseeing (outside rush hours). Especially useful routes include 2 along the Pest bank of the Danube, and 4 and 6 along the Outer Ring to Moskva tér interchange, where they link with the Várbusz.

HÉV surburban trains These connect Budapest with outlying suburbs and towns. The most useful are the ones to Szentendre (leaving from Batthyány tér) and Gödöllő (from Örs vezér tere).

Fares and tickets Tickets must be bought before boarding public transport and can be purchased at metro stations, some tram stops, and newsstands. Validate tickets at metro entrances and on trams, trains and buses. Note that ticket controls are a regular occurrence – the instant fine is 2,500Ft (Money, ➤ 30); when paid at a BKV office (Budapest Transport Company, www.bkv.hu), 7,000Ft – and children up to age six travel free with an adult. A single ticket costs 185Ft and is valid on the same metro, tram, bus or trolleybus as long as you do not change lines or backtrack. A block of 10/20 tickets is available for 1,665/3145Ft. Transfer tickets (320Ft) allow one line change within 1.5 hours. Tickets covering metro travel only are also available; a section ticket costs 130Ft and is valid for three stops

within 30 minutes; a section transfer ticket for 200Ft covers five stops and a change at Deák Ferenc tér within one hour. A transfer ticket for 300Ft allows unlimited stations and one change within the hour.
The simplest solution is a one-day ticket (napijegy, 1150Ft), three-day tourist ticket (touristajegy, 2500Ft), or seven-day travelcard (hetijegy, 3400Ft). Each allows unlimited travel on all forms of BKV transport (except ferries). Fortnightly (4900Ft) and monthly (6900Ft) passes are also available but a photo is required to purchase them.

TAXIS

Be careful of rogue taxis that do not display signs.
Recommended are:
Budataxi ☎ 233 3333; Citytaxi ☎ 211 1111; Fötaxi ☎ 222 2222; Rádiotaxi ☎ 377 7777; Tele3 ☎ 355 5555; Volantaxi ☎ 266 6666.

DRIVING

- Speed limit on motorways (highways): 130kph (80mph)
- Speed limit on major roads: 100kph (60mph). Other roads: 90kph (56mph). Cars with trailers/coaches: 70kph (43mph)
- Speed limit in built-up areas: 50kph (30mph)
- Seat belts must be worn in front seats and rear seats where fitted.
- There is a total alcohol ban for drivers in Hungary.
- Petrol (leaded and unleaded) is readily available. Opening times vary, but there are 24-hour stations. Self-service is the norm. Credit cards are not accepted everywhere.
- Contact the Hungarian Automobile Club (☎ 212 2821, 24-hour service). In the case of an accident call the police (☎ 107) immediately. Assistance with insurance can be obtained from the Allianz Hungária Biztosíto Rt., 1054 Budapest, Bajcsy Zs út 52 ☎ 301 6565.
- Vehicles with damaged bodywork may only leave the country if they have an official certificate.

CAR RENTAL

International car-rental firms have arrangements with local travel agencies, and rental cars are available through them. Avis, is linked with Ibusz, whose 90 offices cover the whole country. The driver must be over 21 and have held a licence for more than one year.

Being there

TOURIST OFFICES

National Tourist Information Centre (Tourinform)
- Sütő utca 2, Budapest V
  (near Deák tér Metro Station)
  ☎ 438 8080;
  www.tourinform.hu
- Liszt Ferenc tér 11,
  Budapest VI ☎ 322 4098

Touchscreen Information
- Tourinform offices
- Ferihegy Airport

Tourism Office of Budapest
- Nyugati Railway Station
  Teréz körút 55, VI
  Main Concourse ☎ 302 8580
- Vár-hegy Szentháromság tér I
  ☎ 488 0475

- Déli Railway Station
- Astoria Metro Station
- Grand Market Hall

MONEY

The monetary unit of Hungary is the forint (HUF). Coins are in denominations of 1, 2, 5, 10, 20, 50 and 100 forints. Most purchases involve the use of banknotes, which come in denominations of 200, 500,1,000, 2,000, 5,000, 10,000 and 20,000 forints.

Travellers' cheques and convertible currency can be changed in banks, travel offices and hotels and credit cards are in increasing use, but by no means everywhere. Eurocheques may be used up to a limit of 30,000 forints. ATMs are widely available.

TIPS/GRATUITIES

Yes ✓ No ✗		
Hotels (if service not included)	✓	10 %
Restaurants (if service not included)	✓	10–20%
Cafés/bars	✓	10%
Taxis	✓	10%
Hairdressers	✓	10–15%
Usherettes	✓	change
Cloakroom attendants	✓	change
Toilets	✓	change
Garage attendants	✓	change

POSTAL AND INTERNET SERVICES

The city's main post office is at Petőfi Sándor utca 13-15, Budapest V,
(🕓 Mon–Fri 8–8, Sat 8–2). Nyugati train station post office is at VI. Teréz
körút 51-53 (🕓 Mon–Sat 7am–9pm, Sun 10–5).

Budapest is dotted with internet cafés, all shopping malls contain one,
A number of bars, restaurants, and cafés provide wi-fi free of charge.

TELEPHONES

Public telephones are widely available. Most accept phonecards rather
than coins. Phonecards can be bought at hotels, newsagents, petrol
stations, tobacconists and post offices.

For local calls, dial the number required. For inland calls dial 06, the area
code and number. For international calls, dial 00, the country access code,
the area code (minus any initial '0') and the number.

The country code to call into Hungary from abroad is 36, followed by 1
for Budapest numbers.

International dialling codes

From Hungary to:	USA and Canada: 00 1
UK: 00 44	Netherlands: 00 31
Germany: 00 49	Spain: 00 34

Emergency telephone numbers

Police: 107	Ambulance: 104
Fire: 105	

EMBASSIES AND CONSULATES

UK ☎ (1) 266 2888	Netherlands ☎ (1) 336 6300
Germany ☎ (1) 488 3505	Spain ☎ (1) 202 4006
USA ☎ (1) 475 4400	

HEALTH ADVICE

Sun advice During summer temperatures can rise to 30°C (85°F) with
bright sunshine. Wear a sunhat and cover your skin as Budapest can
receive around nine hours of sunshine in July and August.

Drugs Pharmacies (*gyógyszertár* or *patika*) issue a wide range of drugs.
Take special medication with you.

Safe water Tap water is safe to drink. Otherwise, bottled water is widely
available. Look for *ásvány víz* (mineral water) or *szóda víz* (soda water).

PERSONAL SAFETY

Security in Budapest is no worse than in any other foreign capital. The most frequent crimes are pickpocketing, confidence tricks and car theft. Tourist Police and uniformed guards, accompanied by interpreters, patrol main tourist areas from July to August.

- Avoid street vendors and beggars.
- Beware of attractive offers.
- Don't carry too much cash.
- Never leave valuables in your car.

Victims of crime should contact the call the English-language crime hotline (24 hours) ☎ 438 8080 🕑 8am–8pm and ☎ 06 80 660 044 🕑 8pm–8am.

ELECTRICITY

The power supply is 220 volts AC. Sockets accept two-pin round plugs, so an adaptor is needed for most non-continental European appliances, and a transformer for appliances operating on 100–120 volts.

OPENING HOURS

- Shops
- Banks
- Attractions/Museums
- Post offices
- Pharmacies

9 AM	10 AM	11 AM	12 PM	1 PM	2 PM	3 PM	4 PM	5 PM	6 PM
9.30	10.30	11.30	12.30	1.30	2.30	3.30	4.30	5.30	

Shops close early on Saturday afternoons, few shops remain open after 1pm. Stores are open late (7–8pm) on Thursdays. Supermarkets and other food shops have longer hours and are open on Sunday mornings. Shops in malls and in areas frequented by tourists also have longer hours and are open on Sundays. Pharmacies follow shop hours but there is always one open late in each area. Banks close early (1pm) on Fridays.

The majority of museums are closed Monday; in winter they usually close earlier. Large churches are open throughout the day, in small towns and villages they may only open early morning and/or evening (6–9pm).

LANGUAGE

Hungarian (Magyar) belongs to the Finno-Ugric group and lies outside the mainstream of European languages. While its spellings are logical, understanding and speaking it pose considerable difficulties to foreigners. Guesswork and improvisation can lead to considerable confusion. English is gradually replacing German as the principal second language, especially among the young. Locals in service industries usually speak German and/or English, and hotel staff may understand several languages.

do you speak English?	*beszél angolul?*	good morning/ night	*jó regggelt/éjszakát*
I don't understand	*nem értem*	goodbye	*viszontlátásra*
yes	*igen*	please	*kérem*
no/not	*nem*	thank you	*köszönöm*
hotel	*szálloda*	per person/per room	*egy személyre/ egy szoba ára*
room	*szoba*		
single/double	*egyágyas/francia ágyas*	reservation	*foglalás*
		rate	*szobaár*
one/two nights	*egy/kettő ejszakra*	breakfast	*regbeli*
bank	*bank*	foreign exchange	*külföldi deviza*
exchange office	*pénzváltó*	foreign currency	*külföldi valuta*
post office	*posta*	pound sterling	*font*
cashier	*pénztáros*	US dollar	*dollár*
restaurant	*étterem*	wine list	*bor lista*
café	*kávéház*	lunch	*ebéd*
table	*asztal*	dinner	*vacsora*
menu	*menükartya*	starter	*előétel*
set menu	*menu*	main course	*főétel*
aeroplane	*repülőgép*	ferry terminal	*komp kikötő*
airport	*repülőtér*	ticket	*jegy*
train	*vonat*	single/return	*egyirányú/retur*
station	*állomás*	first/second class	*első/ másodosztályő*
bus station	*busz allomás*	ticket office	*jegy pénztár*

Best places to see

1 Budai Királyi Palota (Buda Royal Palace)

By far the most grandiose building in Buda, yet ironically a palace whose royals have never been resident, only visiting guests.

No other building in Buda reflects so dramatically the turbulent history of the Castle District. Built in the second half of the 13th century by King Bela IV, after the invasion of the Mongols, centuries of war, invasion and revolution have left little of the palace's original architecture. Razed to the ground during World War II, it was later rebuilt in baroque style.

A magnificent stairway leads to the entrance of the palace proper, where the steep east wall widens into the deep embrasure. Note the statue of Prince Eugene of Savoy, leader of the military operations that forced the Turks finally to retreat.

The double middle wing of the palace, including the dome, houses the National Gallery (➤ 79), with its comprehensive collection of Hungarian painting and sculpture. To reach the other museums, walk through the narrow passage to the west side through a pretty garden square, where you will see the Matthias Well (depicting King Matthias in a hunting scene), regarded as one of the most beautiful fountains in Budapest (➤ 79). The west wing houses the National Széchényi Library

(➤ 80), with its collection of about 7 million works in the form of books, manuscripts, magazines and periodicals.

At the south end of the courtyard is the entrance to the Budapest History Museum (➤ 78), where 2,000 years of the city's history are presented, including the marvellous Renaissance stone collection, which illustrates the former lavishness of the Palace of Matthias Corvinus.

Facing the museum's entrance is a glass door beyond which lies a steep flight of stairs. All that remains, or was possible to recover and reconstruct of the medieval royal castle and fortress, can be seen in the basement. You may by this time feel inclined to spend a little time in the Hsölo (cooling off chamber) situated under the Great Hall – these are cellars where the king's courtiers came to get out of the hot sun.

In the grounds of the royal palace, and worth a closer look in themselves, are the lions that guard the entrance of Oroszlános udvar (The Lion Courtyard), designed by János Fadrusz in 1904. With their grim looks, two of these stone animals seem intent on discouraging visitors. Those brave enough to enter the lions' den are then met by two more inside the gate, roaring angrily. The huge door in the gateway between the lions leads to an elevator which takes you down to the bottom of the wing overlooking Buda.

➕ 3J ✉ Szent György tér, Budapest 1 🕓 Daily throughout the year. Museums daily 10–6 🍴 Rivalda (➤ 100)
🚌 Bus: 16, Várbusz; funicular from Clark Ádám tér
✋ Museums: free or inexpensive

2 Gellért-hegy (Gellért Hill)

Rising to a height of 230m (755ft) between Erzsébet (Elizabeth) and Szabadság (Liberty) bridges over the Danube, this is perhaps the best vantage point from which to see Budapest.

Named after Bishop Gellért (Gerard), who was given the unenviable task of converting the reluctant Magyars to Christianity, this hill provides a commanding view of Budapest, and overlooks the Elizabeth Bridge from which, according to legend, the bishop was cast into the Danube by a bunch of stubborn heathens.

At the foot of the hill are the Rudas Gyogyfürdő (Rudas baths) with their unmistakable domed roof, and inside, an octagonal pool. Crowning the hill is the Citadella (➤ 106), a white stone fortress built to restore order in the aftermath of the 1848–49 War of Independence. Today, as a restaurant, hotel and wax museum, it fortifies nothing more than the hungry and foot-weary.

The top of the hill is crowned by the Szabadság szobor (➤ 109), a striking statue of a woman holding a palm branch aloft. It was raised by the Russians in 1947 and originally incorporated a Soviet soldier, complete with red flag – tactfully removed after the collapse of Communism to the Szoborpark (➤ 175).

Towards Liberty Bridge you can see the famous Gellért Hotel (➤ 107), once the headquarters of the authoritarian regent Admiral Horthy. Now the houses and apartments of the well-heeled dominate this area.

✚ 4L ✉ Budapest I, XI 🕐 Open access 🍴 Restaurant (€€)
🚌 Bus: 27; tram: 18, 19, 47, 49 ✋ Citadel: inexpensive

3 Halászbástya (Fishermen's Bastion)

'We have just seen its replica at the
confectionery exhibition, only slightly
more sugary than the original. While
the tourists are at the dinnertable,
Halászbástya is visited by teenage
couples on their first kiss'.
(András Török, *Budapest, A Critical Guide*)

A Disneyesque edifice situated on the eastern
edge of Castle Hill, the Halászbástya, named after
the fishermen's guild that defended the area in the
Middle Ages, is one of Budapest's most eccentric
structures. Affectedly Gothic in style, it owes more,
perhaps, to the precocious imagination of its
Hungarian architect, Frigyes Schulek, than to any
serious architectural tradition.

Its seven conical towers represent the tents of
the seven Magyar tribes who followed King Árpád
into modern-day Hungary in the 9th century AD,
founding the Magyar kindgom.

The bastion was built as a viewing platform in
1905 during renovations to Mátyás-templom
(Matthias Church ➤ 46–47) and its surrounds –
and what a view it provides. There's no escaping,
or denying, the exceptional vista from its top
ramparts, which take in Pest, the Danube,
Margit-sziget (Margaret Island ➤ 44–45) and
the city's string of bridges. Looking over to Pest,
Szent István Bazilika (Basilica of St Stephen
➤ 44–45) demands the attention of any viewer,
but it's the Országház (Parliament ➤ 48–49) that
steals the architectural show.

Nearby in the Budai Királyi Palota (Buda Royal Palace ➤ 36) is the Magyar Nemzeti Galéria (Hungarian National Gallery ➤ 160) which contains four floors filled with magnificent Hungarian cultural artefacts, including altar-pieces, wood panels, paintings dating from the 13th to the 16th centuries, as well as works by modern and contemporary artists. A truly edifying contrast to the architectural absurdity of the bastion.

✚ 2H 🖂 Szentháromság tér, Budapest I 🕓 Open access
🍴 Ruszwurm (➤ 102) 🚌 Bus: 16, Várbusz; funicular 💷 Free

4 Magyar Állami Operaház (Hungarian State Opera House)

www.opera.hu

Among the most beautiful opera houses in Europe, the opulence of the Opera may distract you from the performance.

Commissioned by the Emperor Franz Joseph, the State Opera House was begun in 1875 under the close supervision of architect Miklós Ybl who apparently checked every cartload of stone. Italian-Renaissance in style, its interior is voluptuously marbled, gilded and decorated with frescoes by some of the finest painters of the time. It opened in 1884 and attracted the biggest names in opera. Gustav Mahler was music director for a time, and after World War II Otto Klemperer took up the directorship. On the stone cornice of the terrace are statues of composers including Mozart, Verdi, Wagner and Beethoven; but niches by the main entrance are reserved for the great 19th-century Hungarian composers Erkel and Liszt. Above the vast auditorium, seating 1,289 people, hangs a three-tonne bronze chandelier decorated with a fine fresco by Károly Lotz.

Despite its *fin de siècle* atmosphere, it is an entirely 'modern' building with all-metal hydraulic stage machinery, an iron curtain and even a sprinkler system. After renovations, the opera house reopened in all its magnificence in 1984, exactly 100 years after the first performance here.

This building is a real treat, and likely to be a highlight of your itinerary. Tickets for performances are available from the box office, but beware: not all seats in the auditorium offer views of the stage.

🚇 5G ✉ Andrássy út 22, Budapest VI ☎ 353 0170; Box office: 332 7914 🕐 Guided tours: Mon–Sun 3 and 4. Box office: Mon–Sat 11–7, Sun 4–7 🍴 Belcanto (➤ 152) Ⓜ M1 Opera 🚌 Bus: 4, red 4 💲 Guided tour: expensive. Performance: regular but not daily

5 Margit-sziget (Margaret Island)

Adrift in the Danube, this idyllic island is the perfect escape from the hustle and bustle of the city.

Citizens of Pest will claim, quite justifiably, that Margaret Island in the Danube is one of Europe's first parks. While not large by city park standards – its length can be strolled in about two hours – it's worth allowing plenty of time for leisurely exploration. It was originally three islands, and the Romans built the first bridge to connect them with the Buda shore. The largest island was called Rabbit Island, reflecting its status as a royal hunting reserve. Its present name was given in honour of King Béla's daughter Margit, who retired to a nunnery there in 1252, at the age of nine. During the Turkish occupation it was home to a harem.

Credit must go to the Habsburg gardeners who planted many of the 10,000 and more trees on the island, most of them plane trees. Here, but under an oak tree, poet János Arany (1817–82) composed 'Under the Oak Trees'.

There are various amenities on the island, including swimming pools, a theatre, zoo, rose garden and Japanese garden, as well as a plethora of statues. At the northern end is the famous old Grand Hotel (now the Danubius Grand Hotel Margitsziget), where the terrace is a pleasant place in which to relax and enjoy the tranquil atmosphere.

✚ 4B ✉ River Danube – between Árpád and Margaret bridges, Budapest XIII ✪ Open access 🍴 Danubius Grand Hotel Margitsziget (➤ 92) 🚌 Bus: 26; tram: 4, 6 💷 Free ❓ Access by car from Árpád Bridge and then only as far as the car park next to the Grand Hotel Margitsziget, otherwise cars prohibited on the island

6 Mátyás-templom (Matthias Church)

www.matyas-templom.hu

Some claim this as a masterpiece of European eclecticism, while others compare it to over-decorated stage scenery.

Originally the place of worship of the German burghers, and dedicated to the Blessed Virgin in Buda, the church owes its popular name to the fact that the legendary Hungarian king Mátyás (Matthias Corvinus, 1458–90) held both his weddings here. Parts date from the 13th century, but the main body of the church was extensively rebuilt in the 19th century. The dazzling, but muted, interior – the result of extensive restoration work carried out by Frigyes Schulek between 1874 and 1896 – recalls many of the original medieval designs. Note the beautiful floral motifs and geometric patterns on the walls. The Turks turned the building into a mosque, and later it was converted into a baroque church. Schulek's dream was to restore it to as much of its original condition as possible, though his enthusiasm for the ornate is all too evident, especially in the spectacular 80m (262ft) high spire.

Enter the church through the Mary Portal where you can see a 14th-century relief depicting the death of the Virgin. In the Loreto Chapel, to the left of the Mary Portal, is a Gothic triptych and a baroque black Madonna dating from 1700. By the main altar hangs the original coat of arms of Matthias Corvinus ('The Raven' ➤ 80). Two chapels, one dedicated to St Imre (son of St Stephen, the first Christian king of Hungary); the other, the Trinity Chapel, housing the tombs of the 12th-century king Béla III and his wife, Anne of Châtillon, are to be found near the main door. Do not miss the impressive collection of ecclesiastical art, which is displayed in the two oratories.

➕ 2H ✉ Szentháromság tér 2, Budapest I ☎ 355 5657
🕐 Mon–Fri 9–5, Sat 9–1, Sun 1–5 🍴 Ruszwurm (▶ 102)
🚌 Bus: 16, Várbusz; funicular ✋ Moderate; includes collection of ecclesiatical art

7 Országház (Parliament)

Budapest's magnificent Parliament building is a vivid expression of Hungarian national identity.

A glorious neo-Gothic edifice with many towers and pinnacles, the building was started in 1884, and completed in 1902. Today it remains a symbol of pride in the independent kingdom, and a testament to the wealth of Hungary's industrial age.

The huge central dome is exactly 96m (315ft) high – a deliberate reference to the Magyar conquest of Hungary in AD896. It dominates a structure that encompasses ten courtyards and 691 rooms.

Directly beneath the dome is a grand 16-sided hall, flanked to the north and south by chambers for the two houses of the Hungarian Parliament (now a single National Assembly). Statues occupy the central hall (a bust of the Parliament's architect Imre Steidl stands modestly off the main staircase), which is still used for state occasions. Additional statues of rulers and military leaders adorn the outside of the building, reinforcing the impression of a strong national identity.

Not everyone admires the building, but for many it is the most outstanding example of neo-Gothic architecture on a grand scale to be seen in the whole of Europe.

Tours of the Parliament pass through the Congress Hall, the main staircase, and the Domed Hall where the country's most valuable item, Szent István's crown, is displayed alongside other precious objects.

➕ 3F ✉ Kossuth Lajos tér 1–3, Budapest V
☎ Tours: 441 4904 🕔 Guided tours (in English): Daily 10am, noon, 2pm; curtailed during parliamentary sessions
🍴 Iguana Bar and Grill (➤ 129) 🚇 M2 Kossuth Lajos tér 🚌 Bus: 15; tram: 2; trolley bus: 70, 78 💶 Free (EU citizens); expensive (non-EU citizens)

8 Szent István Bazilika (St Stephen's Basilica)

The vicissitudes of its construction might well have tested even the patience of God himself, for this basilica took 55 years to build.

This huge church, the largest in the city, holds 8,500 people. Construction started in 1851 but wasn't completed until 1905. The ground plan of the basilica represents the shape of a Greek cross, and is divided into nine barrel-vaulted parts, with a cupola in the middle. No expense was spared: 41kg (90lbs) of 24-carat gold were used for the gilding, while 88 statues adorn the exterior, celebrating, on the Danube side, the Hungarian rulers, and on the Kossuth side, the princes of Transylvania and several famous commanders.

The interior is ornamented with paintings, tapestries, sculptures and frescoes by major Hungarian artists: Mór Thán, Bertalan Székely, Gyula Benczúr, Károly Lotz, Alajos Stróbl, János Fadrusz, Pai Pátzay and Beni Ferenczy.

St Stephen is the country's patron saint. Crowned king of Hungary in 1000, it was Stephen who accepted Christianity, thus bringing his country into the community of Europe. The *Szent Jobb*, his mummified right hand, is preserved in a richly ornamented glass case in

one of the chapels. It is the Hungarian Roman Catholic Church's most revered relic, carried in procession every St Stephen's Day (20 August).

Many important documents and art treasures were stored in the cellars for their protection during the siege of Budapest in early 1945. A long-term restoration programme begun in 1980 has returned the great building to its original pristine appearance. Climb to the dome for fine views over the city.

🚼 5H ✉ Szent István tér, Budapest V ☎ 311 0839
🕐 Mon–Fri 9–5, Sat 9–1, Sun 1–5. Treasury: Apr–Sep daily 9–5; Oct–Mar daily 10–4. Dome: Apr–May daily 10–4:30; Jun–Aug daily 9:30–6; Sep–Oct daily 10–5:30
🍴 Café Kör (► 128)
🚇 M3 Arany János utca, M1 Bajcsy-Zsilinsky út, M1/2/3 Déak Ferenc út ✋ Free

9 Szépművészeti Múzeum (Fine Arts Museum)

If any institution demonstrates Hungarians' appreciation of high art, it is this museum, which ranks as one of the major galleries in Central Europe.

With some 120,000 exhibits, the Fine Arts Museum holds the country's finest collection of foreign art. The designers, Albert Schickedanz and Fölöp Herzog, completed its construction in 1906, and it represents the last piece of eclectic architecture in Hungary. The museum is ideally located in Heroes' Square (➤ 148), which is the grandest of Budapest's many open areas.

The Old Masters Gallery of the museum is world famous, exhibiting works by Raphael, Breughel, Rembrandt, El Greco, Velázquez and Goya, along with many more of the greats. British painting is well represented by Hogarth, Reynolds and Gainsborough. Also here are the French Impressionists and post-Impressionists, including works by Delacroix, Courbet, Millet, Gauguin, Renoir, Monet, Cézanne and Toulouse-Lautrec. Picasso, Chagall, Le Corbusier and Vasarely bring the French collection into the 20th century.

If you haven't had enough by this time, there's also the Ancient Egyptian art collection, which

includes painted wooden mummy cases, 4th-century BC temple reliefs and some fine statuary. If you're a glutton for art, be sure to take in the Greco-Roman collection and also the superb ceramics dating from the 6th to the 1st centuries BC.

There is an enormous amount to get through in this collection, so you may wish to browse through some parts and concentrate on others.

🚩 9P ✉ Dózsa György út 41, Budapest XIV ☎ 469 7100
🕓 Tue–Sun 10–5:30 🍴 Bagolyvàr (▶ 152) 🚇 M1 Hösök
tere 🚌 Bus: 4, 20, 30; trolley bus: 75, 79 🎟 Free ❓ Guided
tours (in English): Tue–Fri 11. Charge for camera and video use

10 Vár-hegy (Castle Hill)

Set on a limestone outcrop overlooking the River Danube, this old residential quarter of Buda is a place of unrivalled charm.

Though the area dates from medieval times and earlier, little remains from this era – the result of successive wars and occupation by foreign powers. Painstaking reconstruction since World War II, when it was virtually destroyed, has, however, restored this part of Buda to a semblance of its once elegant baroque past. The wall of the castle is, in general, well preserved and offers a fine walk and spectacular views. Situated near the wall, close to Holy Trinity Column, is the statue of András Hadik (1710–90), 'the most hussar of hussars', and the commander of Buda Castle. Close inspection of his horse's rear end reveals that its testicles are shiny yellow. Touched by generations of students – allegedly they bring good luck!

Houses 18, 20 and 22 on Országház utca (street), built in the 14th and 15th centuries, show what the Castle District might originally have looked like in medieval times, while on the corner of Országház ucta and Kapisztrán tér (square) stands Mary Magdalene Tower, once a 13th-century church, and the only one allowed to remain a Christian church during Turkish rule. You will be hard-pressed to avoid the famous Ruszwurm pastry shop on

Szentháromság utca (Trinity Street), whose aromas have teased noses since it opened in 1827.

Museums abound in the area, offering a variety of interesting exhibitions: look for the Hadörténeti Múzeum (Museum of Military History ➤ 82), Telefónia Múzeum (Telephone Museum ➤ 86), Budavári Labirintus (Buda Castle Labyrinth ➤ 77), and Arany Sas Patikamúzeum (Golden Eagle Pharmacy ➤ 76).The Buda Royal Palace (➤ 36) houses the Budapest History Museum (➤ 78), the National Széchenyi Library (➤ 80), as well as the National Gallery (➤ 79).

✚ 1H ✉ Budapest I ⊕ Open access except museums
🍴 Rivalda (➤ 100) 🚌 Bus: 16, Várbusz; funicular
✋ Free; admission charge for some museums (➤ 76–88)

Best things to do

Good places to have lunch

Abszint (€€)
Southern-French cuisine and seating on Andrássy út (► 152).

Café Kör (€€)
Light, simple modern Hungarian alongside international dishes in
uncomplicated surrounds (► 128).

Fatál (€€)
Comforting homestyle Hungarian cooking – just the thing on a
winter's day (► 128).

Gundel (€€€)
Hungary's most famous restaurant. Dine in *fin-de-siècle* splendour
on the edge of Városliget (► 153).

Kéhli (€€)
Rustic restaurant with all the traits of rural Hungary (► 99).

Kisbuda Gyöngye (€€)
Fin de siécle salon serving Hungarian specialties (► 99).

Malomtó (€€–€€€)
Stylish restaurant with imaginative international cuisine (► 100).

Menza (€€)
Sit among the retro décor and enjoy all the Hungarian standards
with a modern twist (► 154).

Múzeum (€€)
Quality Hungarian fare in beautifully preserved *fin-de-siècle*
surroundings (► 166).

Robinson (€€)
A perfect lovers' tryst on the lakeside by Heroes' Square (► 154).

Top activities

Take a boat trip on the Danube:
One of the best ways to see the
city (www.mahartpassnave.hu).

Seek out specialist stores:
There's great shopping in Belváros
and along Váci útca (➤ 131–134).

Ride Tram 2: The route along the
Danube banks is a quick and easy
way to catch a glimpse of many of
Budapest's biggest attractions.

Walk around Vár-hegy: Set a day
aside to explore the Castle District
on foot (➤ 54–55).

Go for a stroll: Around car-free
Margit-sziget and the scenic
Budai-hegyek (➤ 44–45,173–174).

Take the waters: A dip in one of
the city's thermal baths is a treat
not to be missed (➤ 66–67).

Spend a night at the opera:
Take in one of the performances
at the Magyar Állami Operáház
(➤ 42–43).

Visit Városliget: The City Park is
a prime picnicking spot (➤ 146).

Places to take the children

VÁR-HEGY, VÍZIVÁROS AND ÓBUDA

Sikló (Funicular) Running between Clark Ádám tér and Buda Royal Palace. The ride lasts only two minutes, but it's fun.
✉ Clark Ádám tér, Budapest ☎ 201 9128 🕐 Daily 7:30am–10pm. Closed 1st and 3rd Mon 🚌 Bus: 16; tram: 19 💷 Inexpensive–moderate

TÉREZVÁROS, ERZSÉBETVÁROS AND VÁROSLIGET

Állatkert (Municipal Zoo) One of the oldest zoos in the world, housing an inordinate number of animals, and 1,500 plant species.
✉ Állatkerti Körút 6–12, Budapest XIV ☎ 273 4901 🕐 May–Aug Mon–Thu 9–6:30, Fri–Sun 9–7; Apr, Sep Mon–Thu 9–5:30, Fri–Sun 9–6; Mar, Oct Mon–Thu 9–5, Fri–Sun 9–5.30; Nov–Feb daily 9–4 🚇 M1 Széchenyi fürdő 🚌 Bus: 724 💷 Expensive

Budapesti Bábszínház (Budapest Puppet Theatre) The puppet shows here are usually in Hungarian but children seem to love them all the same. ✉ Andrássy út 69, Budapest VI ☎ 322 5051 🕐 Shows usually Mon–Fri 10 and 4 🚇 M1 Vörösmarty utca 💷 Moderate

Fővárosi Nagycirkusz (Municipal Circus) World-famous Hungarian trapeze artists, plus clowns and animals.
✉ Állatkerti Körút 12, Budapest XIV ☎ 344 6008 🕐 Shows Wed–Sun 3, also Sat–Sun 10:30, Sun 7 🚇 M1 Széchenyi fürdő 🚌 Bus: 72 💷 Expensive

Vidámpark (Amusement Park) All the usual funfair attractions, plus a restored 19th-century carousel.
✉ Állatkeri Körút 14–16, Budapest XIV ☎ 363 8310 🕐 Apr–Sep daily 10–8; Oct–Mar Sat, Sun 10–7 🚇 M1 Széchenyi fürdő 🚌 Bus: 72 💷 Inexpensive

JÓZSEFVAROS AND FERENCVÁROS

Csodák Palotája: Interaktív Tudományos Játszóház (Palace of Miracles: Interactive Scientific Playhouse)
Behind the extensive name are over 100 spectacular, hands-on games and experiments.

✉ Fény utca 20–22, Budapest II ☎ 350 6131 ⏰ Jul–Aug daily 10–6;
Sep–Jun Mon–Fri, 9–5, Sat–Sun 10–6 🚇 M2 Moszkva tér ✋ Moderate

Planetárium The largest Hungarian institution of public education
on space exploration and astronomy.

✉ Népliget, Budapest X
☎ 263 1811 ⏰ Tue–Sun 9–4;
extra shows Wed, Thu 5:30
🚇 M3 Népliget ✋ Moderate

BUDAI-HEGYEK
Gyermekvasút
(Children's Railway)

Narrow-gauge railway
running along an 11km (8-
mile) route and supervised
(in additon to the driver) by
uniformed local children.
The train calls at János Hill,
the city's highest point.

✉ Hegyhát út Budapest X
☎ 397 5392 ⏰ Mid-Mar to Oct
Mon–Fri 10–5, Sat, Sun
9:45–5:30; Nov to mid-Mar
Tue–Fri 10–4, Sat–Sun 10–5
🚋 Tram: 56
✋ One-way: inexpensive;
round-trip: moderate

Libegő (Chairlift)

The 15-minute trip between Zugliget and János Hill offers
unforgettable views.

✉ Zugligeti út 93, Budapest ⏰ Mid-May to mid-Sep daily 9:30–5; mid-Sep
to mid-May daily 9:30–4:30 🚇 Moszkva tér, then bus 158 ✋ Inexpensive

a walk around Nagykörút (Grand Boulevard)

This is the longest thoroughfare of the city, running from Petőfi híd in the south to Margit híd in the north. It changes names five times along the way, representing the five districts it traverses; Ferenc körút in district IX, József körút in VIII, Erzsébet körút in VII, Teréz körút in VI, and Szent István körút in XIII.

Start at Boráros tér by the Petőfi Bridge heading towards Ferenc körút.

On your left are three large blocks of pre-World War II apartments and between them on Bakats tér the beautiful spired Ferencváros Parish Church.

Continue up Ferenc körút to Üllői út and the Museum of Applied Arts (▶ 162). Cross Üllői út, and on your right is the Corvin Cinema, the headquarters of armed resistance during the 1956 Uprising. Now you're on Jósef körút. On your way to Rákóczi tér, on the right, look out for the War Memorial.

Rákóczi tér, once a playground for Budapest's seedier side, has been cleaned up somewhat but still retains a semblance of colour.

Farther on up the tree-lined boulevard, on the right, is Blaha Lujza tér, one of the city's central squares. Cross Rákóczi út, and head for the New York café, restored to its original glory. Now you're on Erzsébet körút. The Grand Hotel Royal is on your right. A short walk farther on is Teréz körút with the magnificent Academy of Music (➤ 141).

On the right where Andrássy út joins the Oktogon is the copy of Florentine Palazzo Strozz.

A little farther on, with the Hotel Béke Radisson on the right, you arrive at Nyugati tér with the finely restored Western Railway Station (➤ 139). Cross Szent István körút. On your right, at Szent István körút, is the Vígszínház theatre. A short walk along on the right takes you to Margaret Bridge and the Danube.

Distance 4km (3.5 miles)
Time 4–5 hours, 6 hours with stops
Start point Boráros tér ✚ 8X 🚊 Tram: 2
End point Margít híd (Margaret Bridge) ✚ 3E 🚊 Tram: 2
Lunch Café New York ✉ Erzsébet Körút 9–11 ☎ 322 3849

Best thermal baths

Csillaghegy

The city's oldest open-air bath, with three pools and parkland.

✉ Pusztakúti út 3, Budapest III ☎ 250 1533 🚌 HÉV Csillaghegy
✋ Expensive

Dagály

A massive complex with ten pools, some of which are filled with warm thermal water.

✉ Népfürdő utca 36, Budapest XIII ☎ 452 4500 🚇 M3 Árpád híd
✋ Expensive

Gellért
This art nouveau gem has both indoor and outdoor pools (➤ 107).

Király
Király has a wonderful sky-lit cupola (➤ 92).

Lukács
The neoclassical complex with Turkish origins has indoor and outdoor thermal pools, and its sulphuric waters can be taken.
✉ Frankel Leó utca 25–29, Budapest II ☎ 326 1695 🚌 Bus: 86
✋ Expensive

Rác
Original Turkish bath with a 19th-century façade undergoing extensive renovation to create a luxury hotel spa complex.
✉ Hadnagy utca 8–10, Budapest I 🚃 Tram: 18, 19

Rudas
A classic Turkish bath dating from 1566, Rudas offers a domed octagonal room, atmospheric surrounds, and a neoclassical wing.
✉ Döbrentei tér 9, Budapest I ☎ 356 1322 🚃 Tram: 18, 19; bus: 7
✋ Swimming pool moderate, thermal baths expensive

Széchenyi
Neoclassical in design, Széchenyi is a gorgeous outdoor arena with its fair share of indoor pools and thermal treatments (➤ 147).

Thermal
Thermal is a modern spa connected to the Grand Hotel Margit-sziget (➤ 96), in a lovely setting on Budapest's favourite island.
✉ Margit-sziget, Budapest XIII ☎ 889 4737 🚌 Bus: 26 ✋ Expensive

Stunning views

From Vár-hegy (Castle Hill ➤ 54), particularly from Halászbástya (Fishermen's Bastion, ➤ 40).

From Gellért-hegy (Gellért Hill ➤ 38) over Pest and Vár-hegy.

From Árpád híd for views of the city and river (➤ 94).

From Erzsébet-kiláto (Elizabeth tower) on Janos-hegy (➤ 174).

From the dome of Szent István Bazilika (St Stephen's Basilica ➤ 50).

From the terrace of the Bellevue Restaurant, Mariott Hotel.

From the Watertower on Margit-sziget (Marget Island ➤ 44).

From Vienna Gate (➤ 76) at the northern end of Vár-hegy.

From Dunakorzó (➤ 117) across to Buda and its Danube embankment.

From Tram 2 along the Pest embankment.

Best art nouveau

Állatkert (Zoo) The entranceway and elephant house of the Állatkert are unmistakable examples of art nouveau (► 62).

Bedő Ház (Bedő House) Not an extravagant structure, but its unusual façade, with flower designs, grumpy faces, and individual window frames, is highly appealing. ✉ Honvéd utca 3, Budapest V

Földtani Intézet (Geology Institute) Look for its mesmerizing blue-tiled roof and stunning interior. ✉ Stefánia út 14, Budapest XIV

Gresham Palace A beautifully restored example of secessionist (Hungarian art nouveau) architecture (► 122).

Gellért Gyógyfürdő (Gellért Thermal Baths) One of the few examples of art nouveau on the Buda side of the river (► 107).

Iparművészeti Múzeum (Museum of Applied Arts) Features an exterior of Zsolnay ceramic tiles and Moorish design (► 162).

Magyar Királyi Takarék Pénztár (Former Royal Post Office Savings Bank) Hungarian folk art motifs, art nouveau swirls, a lime-green roof, and even a swarm of bees (► 123).

Thonet Ház (Thonet House) Another designed by Ödön Lechner – who is also responsible for the Museum of Applied Arts, the Royal Savings Bank, and the Geology Institute – with generous use of Zsolnay tiles and floral motifs. ✉ Vaci utca 11, Budapest V

Török Bankház (Turkish Bank House) Unexceptional until you encounter its gable, filled with a mosaic by Miksa Róth depicting Hungary paying homage to the Virgin Mary. ✉ Szervita tér 3, Budapest V

Zeneakadémia (Academy of Music) As interiors go, the Zeneakadémia is hard to beat (► 141).

Exploring

Not until 1873, when the two districts of Buda and Pest were amalgamated, did the capital city of Budapest come into existence. The first major settlement here was Aquincum, a civic settlement built by the Romans. Remains of their aqueduct and amphitheatres remain just north of Óbuda. Buda itself, an important centre of Renaissance learning during the 16th century, fell into decline during the 150 years of Turkish occupation. One legacy of the Turks was their thermal baths, which are an unmissable treat. On the eastern bank of the Danube, Pest only came into prominence in the 19th century. Once Hungary had wrested virtual autonomy from the Habsburgs in the Compromise of 1867, this part of the city expanded rapidly to the east of the Danube. By 1896, united Budapest had become a great metropolitan centre, with a thriving cultural life that still reverberates today in a host of venues of all kinds.

Vár-hegy, Víziváros and Óbuda

Nothing in Budapest is as dominant as Vár-hegy (Castle Hill). This lofty limestone plateau rising above the Danube is an arresting sight, topped by a walled medieval town containing some of the city's greatest sights. Between Vár-hegy and the fast-flowing Danube is the Víziváros (Watertown) and to the north lies Óbuda, Budapest's ancient heart.

ÓBUDA

Margit-sziget

VÍZIVÁROS

VÁR-HEGY

Vár-hegy is home to the former Hungarian royal quarters (Budai Királyi Palota ► 36), the unique Mátyás-templom (Matthias Church ► 46), and a good collection of informative and unusual museums.

Simply wandering its quiet, cobblestone streets (only residents can drive here) is as pleasurable as seeing any big attraction.

Nearby Víziváros is a long, thin district with a subdued atmosphere and an intriguing past. Its foundations were laid by the Romans and reminders of the Turkish occupation are dotted throughout the area.

Óbuda also has a long history; while now a quiet corner of the city, it was here that the Romans established the town of Aquincum almost 2000 years ago.

Vár-hegy
Best places to see, ➤ 54–55.

ARANY SAS PATIKAMÚZEUM
(GOLDEN EAGLE PHRARMACY)

Its current neoclassical façade may date from 1820, but the Arany Sas Patikamúzeum occupies a 15th-century building in the heart of the Castle District. It is the first pharmacy established in Buda after the expulsion of the Turks and contains an unusual collection of archaic pharmaceutical paraphernalia, including mummy powder reputed to cure epilepsy, dried bats and a mock laboratory. Note the painting of the nun – during the Middle Ages it was their job to perform the task of a chemist.

➕ 2H ✉ Tárnok utca 18, Budapest I ☎ 375 9772 ⏱ Apr–Oct Tue–Sun 10:30–6; Nov–Mar Tue–Sun 10:30–4 🍴 Ruszwurm (€) ♿ Free 🚌 Bus: 16

BÉCSI KAPU
(VIENNA GATE)

The Vienna Gate is where all four streets that run the length of Castle Hill converge, and in the Middle Ages this was the place of the 'Saturday Market' for non-Jewish merchant traders. The story goes that any loud-mouthed Hungarian child would be scolded by being told his mouth was 'as big as the Vienna Gate'.

Climb to the top of the gate and enjoy the panorama of Buda and the view of the Lutheran church in the square. There are also fine views of the Parliament building across the Danube. Next to the bastion wall, to the right of the gate, is a small grove, the 'Europe Grove'. It gets its name from the time when the mayors of cities all over Europe brought and planted rare trees here, for example, Turkish hazel, Japanese cherry and cherry laurel.

🚑 1G ✉ Castle District, Budapest I 🕐 Open access 🍴 Café Pierrot (€€) 🚌 Várbusz 👋 Free ❓ Cars are not allowed to enter the Castle District without a permit

BUDAI LABIRINTUS (CASTLE LABYRINTH)

The entrance on Uri utca 9 leads to an underground labyrinth stretching for about 10km (6 miles) beneath Castle Hill. These fascinating caves were joined together by the Turks for military purposes and today a section of about 1.2km (0.75 mile) can be explored. A waxwork exhibition (not to everyone's taste) is located here – a memorial of Hungarian history that is both light-hearted and serious. The exhibition recounts Hungary's mythological beginnings and finishes in the flourishing Renaissance Court of King Matthias. Oddly, nothing of Hungary's more recent, perhaps less glorious, times, is included. Only a street sign on the wall recalls the bitter years of World War II when thousands of people took refuge here from the siege.

Not recommended for those who suffer from claustrophobia.

🚑 2H ✉ Uri utca 9, Budapest I ☎ 489 3281 🕐 Daily 9:30–7:30 🍴 Miro (€) 🚌 Bus: 16, Várbusz; funicular 👋 Expensive ❓ Guided tours only

BUDAI KIRÁLYI PALOTA (BUDA ROYAL PALACE)

Best places to see, ➤ 36–37.

Budapesti Történeti Múzeum (Budapest History Museum)

Occupying the southern end of the Buda Royal Palace, this excellent exhibition provides a historical record of Budapest's last 2,000 years. In the basement front hall of the history museum there's a plaster model of Castle Hill, and a detailed black-and-white drawing of the Gothic Buda Royal Palace as it probably used to be. Its largest hall was 70m (76yds) by 17m (19yds), where even horseback tournaments took place! The museum is divided into two sections. On the lower level (a maze of passageways, cellars and vaulted halls) can be seen the remains of the medieval palace, together with sculptures, pots and pans, and weapons. Above is the principal exhibition, documenting Budapest's long history, and containing photographs, prints and posters and, perhaps surprisingly, surviving artefacts from the Turkish occupation

✚ 3J ✉ Budai Királyi Palota (Wing E), Budapest I ☎ 225 7809 🕓 Mid-May to mid-Sep daily 10–6; Mar to mid-May, mid-Sep to Oct Wed–Mon 10–6; Nov–Feb Wed–Mon 10–4 🍴 Café Pierrot (€€) 🚌 Bus: 16, Várbusz; funicular ♿ Moderate

Mátyás-Kút (Matthias Well)

Placed against a north-facing wall of the Buda Royal Palace, the well has a bronze statue of King Matthias as a huntsman in the company of his shield bearer and Italian chronicler. The statue includes the figure of Szep Ilonka (Helen the Fair), a beautiful peasant girl who fell in love with the king while he was hunting – a case of unrequited love. This impressive statue is well worth seeking out.

🕂 3J 🖂 Szent György tér, Budapest I 🕐 Open access 🍴 Restaurants and cafés nearby (€€) 🚌 Bus: 16, Várbusz; funicular

Magyar Nemzeti Galéria (Hungarian National Gallery)

This huge and richly stocked gallery traces the evolution of the arts in Hungary from the Middle Ages to the 20th century. It's too much to take in at one time; concentrate on a few treasures, such as the medieval altarpieces. Hungarian history is amply illustrated in large canvases of heroic deeds. Perhaps the most appealing sections deal with the late 19th and early 20th centuries, when Hungarian artists made a significant contribution to the

Impressionist and art nouveau movements. Look for words by the sensitive Jósef Rippl-Rónai, while the wayward Tivadar Koszta Csontváry is in his own category, with a highly personal symbolism.

🔢 3J 🖂 Budai Királyi Palota (Wings B, C and D), Budapest I ☎ 06 20 4397 325 🕐 Tue–Sun 10–6 🍴 Restaurants and cafés nearby (€€) 🚌 Bus: 16, Várbusz; funicular 💶 Free; temporary exhibitions moderate ❓ Tours

Országos Széchenyi Könyvtár (National Széchenyi Library)

Yet another major site in the Buda Royal Palace, this library stocks over 2 million books, and even more manuscripts, musical scores and newspapers. Among these are the few remaining codices (manuscript volumes) from King Matthias's celebrated library. The codices are called Corvinas, and refer to the raven – the King's heraldic emblem. The Main Reading Room, made up of several smaller rooms, is spacious but not especially elegant.

🔢 3J 🖂 Budai Királyi Palota (Wing F), Budapest I ☎ 224 3700 🕐 Sep–Jul Tue–Fri 9–9, Sat 10–6. Closed Aug 🍴 Restaurants and cafés nearby (€€) 🚌 Bus: 16, Várbusz; funicular 💶 Moderate

Savoyai Jenő szobor (Statue of Eugene of Savoy)

Opposite the entrance to Buda Royal Palace on the Danube side is the powerful equestrian statue of Prince Eugene of Savoy (1663–1736). Born in Paris, following his father's death and his mother's subsequent banishment from the French court by Louis XIV, the prince renounced the country of his birth and joined the service of Emperor Leopold I in the fight against the Turks. In a distinguished career he inflicted a series of defeats on the Turks; in 1697 at Zenta on the River Tisza, in 1716 at Petrovaradin and Temesvar (now Timisoara), and in 1717 at Belgrade where his force of 40,000 overcame an army of nearly 250,000 and Eugene was wounded for the 13th time.

🔢 3J 🖂 Front entrance, Budai Királyi Palota, Budapest I 🚌 Bus: 16, Várbusz; funicular

HADTÖRTÉNETI MÚZEUM
(MUSEUM OF MILITARY HISTORY)

Facing the Buda Hills is this, the city's museum devoted to
Hungary's military history. While it looks like the kind of museum
where static displays might sit and collect dust, it actually
does a fine job of covering the country's military exploits against
occupying forces and during the two world wars through
uniforms, weapons, and other memorabilia. Special sections on
the 1848–49 revolution and the 1956 Uprising are enlightening,
and the oft-forgotten period just after World War I – when the
'Red Army' travelled through the country acting as a death squad –
is quite shocking. A handful of displays are complimented with
English explanations, and there are tours in English and German.

✚ 1G ✉ Tóth Árpád sétány 40, Budapest I ☎ 325 1651 ⏰ Apr–Sep
Tue–Sun 10–6; Oct–Mar Tue–Sun 10–4 🍴 Café Pierrot (€€) 🚌 Bus: 16
✋ Free

HALÁSZBÁSTYA
(FISHERMEN'S BASTION)

Best places to see, ➤ 40–41.

MÁRIA MAGDOLNA-
TORONY (MARY
MAGDALENE TOWER)

On the corner of Országház utca
and Kapisztrán tér, this 13th-
century church was built for
Hungarian worshippers on the
border of a German parish. During
Turkish rule special dispensation
was given to the church to allow it
to remain Christian, while all other
churches were converted to
mosques. Unfortunately the

chancel and nave were destroyed during World War II, and have not been rebuilt, except for one stone window as a memento. Worthy of note are the serried ranks of 24 bells. Their chime, a modern addition, sounds like tumbling icicles.

✚ 1G ✉ Kapisztrán tér 6, Budapest I 🕐 Daily 10–6 🍴 Restaurants and cafés nearby (€) 🚌 Bus: 16, Várbusz 🎫 Free

MÁTYÁS-TEMPLOM (MATTHIAS CHURCH)

Best places to see, ➤ 46–47.

ORSZÁGHÁZ UTCA 18, 20, 22

Built in the 14th and 15th centuries, these three houses show what the Castle District may have looked like in the Middle Ages. Italian craftsmen working on the Royal Palace once lived here. The initials inscribed on the gate of the middle house are those of Johann Nicki, the butcher who had the house rebuilt in 1771. The rear-view mirror on one of the windows was to allow the person inside to check who was at the front door.

✚ 1G ✉ Országház utca 18, 20, 22, Budapest I 🍴 Miro (€) 🚌 Várbusz

RÉGI BUDAI VÁROSHÁZA (OLD TOWN HALL)

This imposingly quaint building, formerly the seat of the city's council, is now an Institute for Advanced Studies. The first session of the Council was held here in 1710, but its governing function came to an end in 1873 when Buda and Pest were united. The fine proportions of the Old Town Hall's windows and inner forked staircase suggest erstwhile political harmony. The statue (actually an Italian copy) on the corner of the building represents Pallas Athena, the guardian of towns. Reminiscent of some of the smaller Oxford colleges, this is a bustling place during term-time. Don't feel reticent about visiting it during this time, as the students and staff are most welcoming.

➕ 2H ✉ Szentháromság utca 2, Budapest I ⊛ Officially not open to the public, but visitors welcome 🚌 Bus: 16, Varbusz; funicular

SIKLÓ (FUNICULAR)

This is not just worth seeing, but is also fun to ride. Opened to the public in 1870, like the rest of the Castle District it suffered severe damage during World War II, and was rebuilt in 1986. Originally the railway was steam powered and adroitly used the weight of the passengers and car going downwards to pull the other car upwards. You can enjoy a wonderful view of the Pest area from the funicular. The ride from the Buda end of the Chain Bridge up to Castle Hill takes two minutes. The car also carries prams (strollers) and wheelchairs. Buy your tickets there.

➕ 3J ✉ Clark Ádám tér (lower terminus), Szent György tér (upper terminus), Budapest I ⊛ Daily 7:30am–10pm. Closed every other Mon
🚌 Bus: 4, 16; tram: 19 💰 Inexpensive one-way

SZÉCHENYI LÁNCHÍD (SZÉCHENYI CHAIN BRIDGE)

A symbol of Budapest and the first bridge over the Danube, this bridge was built between 1839 and 1849 on the initiative of Count István Széchenyi. It was designed by Englishman William Tierney Clark, and built by his namesake, the Scotsman Adam Clark.

During the country's War of Independence, the first carriage to cross the bridge (at a time when it was still under construction) carried the Hungarian crown from Buda, which was then under siege, to Debrecen. Later, the Austrian troops decided to blow the bridge up – but the ever-resourceful Adam Clark frustrated their attempt by flooding the explosive-packed chain chambers with water. However, the Széchenyi Chain Bridge was eventually blown up during World War II. It reopened again on 20 November 1949, exactly 100 years after its original inauguration.

✠ 3H ✉ Clark Ádám tér, Budapest I to Roosevelt tér, Budapest V 🍴 Seoul House (€) 🚌 Bus: red 4, 16; tram: 2, 19

SZENTHÁROMSÁG SZOBOR
(HOLY TRINITY COLUMN)

Situated in the middle of Szentháromság tér near
Matthias Church, the highest point on Castle Hill, the
14m (46-foot) tall monument was erected between
1710 and 1713 by the inhabitants of Buda. It was
hoped that the column would fend off further plague
epidemics that had sporadically ravaged the city.

✚ 2H ⊠ Szentháromság tér, Budapest I 🍴 Ruszwurm (€)
🚌 Bus: 16, Várbusz

TELEFÓNIA MÚZEUM
(TELEPHONE MUSEUM)

The enlightening little Telephone Museum retells the
history of the phone in Budapest, and in the process
is a startling reminder of the speed at which
technology has developed over just a century.

In 1882, Budapest was the third city in Europe to
install a telephone exchange (after London and Paris),
and the museum premises were used as a secondary
exchange from 1928 to 1985. The huge exchange is
still in working order, and if it's not too busy the ticket
attendant will flip a switch to make it whiz and burr.

A second room houses a number of public phones
(the first was installed in Belváros in 1928) and the
first mobiles; produced by Motorola and Ericsson, the
latter look more like small suitcases than the handy
little devices we use today. Bizarrely, there's also a
small shrine to Gábor Dénes (1900–79), inventor of
the hologram and 1971 Nobel Prize winner. The
museum overlooks a peaceful inner courtyard, which
is a fine spot to escape the castle's summer crowds.

✚ 1G ⊠ Úri utca 9, Budapest I ☎ 201 8188 🕐 Tue–Sun
10–4 ♿ Inexpensive 🚌 Bus: 16

ÚRI UTCA 31 (LORDS' STREET 31)

This endearingly named street in the Castle District has the distinction of being the only row of houses in the area to run in a north–south direction. The façades are later additions, but the courtyards, the ground floors, the gateways with their recessed benches, and the cellars are authentically medieval, and well worth seeing. This is a place where you can literally step into the past – but do it in a genteel way.

➕ 2H ✉ Úri utca, Budapest I 🍴 Miro (€) 🚌 Bus: 16, Várbusz; funicular

VÁRSZÍNHÁZ (CASTLE THEATRE)

Completed in 1736, the building was originally the Church of the Order of Our Lady of Mount Carmel, but in 1784 Joseph II dissolved this order. The monastery then became a casino, and the church gave way to a theatre. The theatre had a wooden floor and could seat 1,200 people, and it was here that the first ever play in Hungarian was performed – all previous performances had been in German. In 1924 a part of the gallery collapsed, postponing the next performance until 1978 when the new theatre, of marble and concrete (seating 264 people), was opened. It houses the Nemezti Táncszínház (National Dance Theatre).

➕ 2H ✉ Színház utca 1–3, Budapest I 🕐 Daily
☎ 201 4407 ☎ 375 8649 🍴 Rivalda (€€€) 🚌 Bus: 16, Várbusz; funicular

a walk around Vár-hegy (Castle Hill)

This walk round Castle Hill (▶ 54) gives a taste of the old town of Buda.

From the cobbled Dísz tér (square) enter Tárnok utca.

At No 18 is the Patikamúzeum (Museum of Pharmacy), a former chemist's shop dating from 1745.

Walk towards Szentháromság tér. Pass to the right of Matthias Church (▶ 46) into cobbled courtyards with the Halászbástya (Fishermen's Bastion ▶ 40) in front of you.

Climb the towers of Fishermen's Bastion for spectacular views of the Danube and Pest.

Return via the north side of Matthias Church with the Hilton Hotel on your right. Back on the Szentháromság tér, turn right into Hess András tér, then bear left and walk down Fortuna utca.

Fortuna utca is perhaps the most picturesque street on Castle Hill.

Passing the Café Pierrot, enter Bécsikapu tér, dominated by the neo-Romanesque edifice of the National Archives of Hungary. Walk up Petermann Bíró utca to the tower and ruins of medieval Mary Magdalene Church (▶ 82) then turn left towards Úri utca.

The pastel-green building on the right, with a police sign outside, houses the Telefónia Múzeum (Telephone Museum ▶ 86).

Return to Szentháromság tér. Turn left by the equestrian statue of Hadik András to Tóth Árpád sétány for distant views of the Buda Hills. Turn back, then right onto Úri utca.

At No 9 is the entrance to the Castle Labyrinth (▶ 77). Many of the caves are believed to be between 500 and 700 years old and were used for military purposes by occupying Turks.

Walk down into Dísz tér, where the walk ends.

Distance Approx 1km (0.6 miles)
Time 1 hour, or 2 hours with stops
Start/end point Disz tér ✚ 2H
🚇 Castle line (signed 'V'), leave from Moszkva tér; Várbusz; funicular from Szent György tér
Lunch Rivalda (€€€) ✉ Színház utca 2 ☎ 489 0236

Víziváros

KIRÁLY GYÓGYFÜRDŐ (KIRÁLY THERMAL BATHS)

One of the most famous thermal baths in Hungary, this is where to come for a course of complete revitalization. Besides the thermal pool, there are tub baths, salt baths and massage and sauna services. Built on a former Roman military road, the baths were constructed by the Turkish Pasha of Buda, Arslan, in the 16th century. It was then bought by the Konig (meaning 'King' in German) family, from which the name Király (meaning 'King' in Hungarian') stems. The building's Turkish decor and styling, especially the cupolas, make it an architectural masterpiece.

✚ 2F ✉ Fő utca 82–4, Budapest II ☎ 202 3688
🍴 Café (€) 🕐 Men: Tue, Thu, Sat 9–8. Women: Mon, Wed, Fri 7–6 🚇 M2 Batthyány tér
🚌 Bus: 60, 86 ✋ Moderate

ÖNTÖDEI MÚZEUM (FOUNDRY MUSEUM)

Built on the site of the old Ganz ironworks, which produced the world's first electric railway engine, the museum contains a reconstructed foundry and workshop, also an interesting collection of products once manufactured here.

🔳 2F 🖂 Bem József utca 20, Budapest II ☎ 202 5011
🕐 Tue–Sun 9–5 🍴 Kacsa (€€) 🚇 M2 Batthyány tér 🚌 Bus: 11, 60, 86; tram: 4, 6 🎟 Free

SZENT ANNA TEMPLOM

St Anne's Church is the finest example of baroque architecture in the city. Commissioned by the Jesuits in 1740, it took another 65 years to be consecrated due to some major delays – it suffered earthquake damage in 1763 and the dissolution of the Jesuit order in 1773, and World War II saw the façade sustain more damage. The highlight of the rich baroque façade is the Buda coat of arms, which is topped by two kneeling angels and the Trinity symbol. Inside, statues of St Anne presenting Mary to the Temple of Jerusalem complement the concave High Altar, which rises to the central frescoed dome. Also of note are the 1768 dark side altar and the cherub-topped organ which once resided in one of Vár-hegy's churches.

🔳 3F 🖂 Batthyány tér 8, Budapest II ☎ 318 5536 🕐 Services: Mon–Fri 7:30am, 9:30am, 5pm, Sat 8:30am, 9:30am, 6pm, Sun 8:30am, 9am, 11am, 6pm 🍴 Angelika (€)
🎟 Inexpensive 🚇 M2 Batthyány tér

Óbuda

AQUINCUM

Once a bustling town established by the Romans in the 1st century AD, Aquincum is today a collection of grassy areas and sectioned ruins. Most of the finds, which were uncovered during excavation in the late 19th century, are housed in the site's museum. Pottery, weapons, jewellery, coins and mosaics are the mainstay of the museum's collection, but keep an eye out for the exceptional water-powered organ that has been restored to working order. Of the scattered ruins, the public baths and Macellum, the town's covered market, are the most intact.

🚌 3A (off map) ✉ Szentendrei út 139, Budapest III ☎ 250 1650 🕐 May–Sep Tue–Sun 9–6; 15–30 Apr, Oct Tue–Sun 9–5 🍴 Café (€) ✋ Moderate 🚇 HÉV Aquincum

ÁRPÁD HÍD (ÁRPÁD BRIDGE)

North of Margaret Bridge, Árpád Bridge is the longest and most robust of the six

bridges crossing the Danube in the vicinity of downtown Budapest and links the mainland with Margaret Island (▶ 44). It's worth a walk across if only for the views it offers of the city and a sense of the immense breadth of the Danube, and Margaret Island is certainly worth a visit.

➕ 6A ✉ Árpád híd, Budapest III
🍴 Kéhli (€€) 🚌 Bus: 26; tram: 1

HERCULES VILLA

The Hercules Villa refers not to a building but to a series of 3rd-century AD mosaic floors discovered hidden among a block of residential flats in the late 1950s. In extremely good condition considering their age, the mosaics depict Hercules firing an arrow into centaur Nessos as he takes flight with Deineira. The detailed work (some 60,000 stones) was probably brought to Buda from Alexandria already arranged and ready to go.

➕ 3A ✉ Meggyfa utca 19–21, Budapest III
☎ 250 1650 🕐 May–Sep Tue–Sun 9–6;
Apr, Oct Tue–Sun 9–5
🍴 Új Sípos Halászkert (€€)
✋ Free 🚌 Bus: 86

MARGIT-SZIGET
(MARGARET ISLAND)

Best places to see, ▶ 44–45.

HOTELS

Aquincum Corinthia (€€)

On the Buda river front, with interesting architectural sites nearby, this takes its Roman name from the first sizeable settlement in the region. This five-star hotel has 312 rooms, some with views across to Margaret Island.

✉ Árpád fejedelem útja, 94, Budapest III ☎ 436 4100; www.corinthiahotels.com

art'otel (€€€)

In the picturesque setting of the Víziváros area between the Danbue and Castle Hill, the 'art hotel' is a wonderful synthesis of immaculately restored 18th-century fishermen's dwellings and 21st-century designer rooms featuring the work of New Yorker Donald Sultan.

✉ Bem rakpart 16–19, Budapest I ☎ 487 9487; www.artotel.de

Buda Center Hotel (€€)

With 34 rooms and 3 family apartments, this hotel is conveniently situated a few minutes away from the city centre at the foot of Castle Hill.

✉ Csalogány út 23, Budapest II ☎ 201 6333

Danubius Grand Hotel Margitsziget (€€€)

Four-star and with 164 rooms, this old spa hotel shares a beautiful setting with the Danubius Thermal Hotel on Margaret Island in the middle of the Danube and a few minutes from the city centre.

✉ Margit-sziget, Budapest XIII ☎ 889 4700; www.danubiusgroup.com

Danubius Thermal Hotel Margitsziget (€€€)

This modern spa hotel is much less elegant than the Danubius Grand (▶ above), but the location on Margaret Island is very attractive, as is its four-star rating. The spa receives natural spring water from the island. There are 206 rooms.

✉ Margit-sziget, Budapest XI11 ☎ 889 4700; www.danubiusgroup.com

Hilton Hotel (€€€)

A pearl in the Hilton chain, this modern 323-room hotel in the Castle District blends tastefully with its picturesque surroundings and, naturally, offers high standards all round including wireless internet access in all rooms.

✉ Hess András tér 1–3, Budapest | ☎ 889 6600; www.budapest.hilton.com

Hotel Budapest (€€€)

A large, modern hotel within walking distance of Castle Hill, this is a conference-oriented hotel, but offers fine views of Buda.

✉ Szilágyi Erzsébet fasor 47, Budapest | ☎ 889 4200; www.danubiusgroup.com

Kulturinnov (€€)

Modest, comfortable dormitory-type rooms. Its attraction is that it is only 200m (220 yards) from Matthias Church in the beautiful Castle District. Some parts are grand, some shabby.

✉ Szentháromság tér 6, Budapest | ☎ 224 8192; www.kulturinnov.hu
🚌 Bus: 16, Várbusz

Mercure Buda (€€)

The hotel is not especially pleasing to look at but the 399 rooms offer good views.

✉ Krisztina körút 41–43, Budapest | ☎ 488 8100; www.mercure-buda.hu

Novotel Budapest Congress (€€)

This hotel is beside the Budapest Convention Centre. Its 324 comfortable rooms and good facilities are let down by its location.

✉ Alkotás utca 63–67, Budapest XII ☎ 372 5400; www.novotel-bud-congress.hu

Orion Hotel (€€)

At the foot of Castle Hill, this hotel has 31 air-conditioned rooms. It has a breakfast room.

✉ Döbrentei utca 13, Budapest | ☎ 356 8583; www.bestwestern-ce.com/orion

Victoria (€€)

On the Buda riverbank, this comfortable 27-room hotel with full facilities overlooks the old Chain Bridge.

✉ Bem rakpart 2, Budapest | ☎ 457 8080; www.victoria.hu 🚌 Bus: 16, tram 19

RESTAURANTS

Alabardos (€€€)

In one of the most venerable buildings on Castle Hill, this refined establishment offers the best in Hungarian cuisine in an elegant candlelit setting.

✉ Országház utca 2, Budapest | ☎ 356 0851 🕐 Lunch Sat, dinner Mon–Sat. Closed Sun

Arany Kaviár (€€)

There is no need to point out that this restaurant specializes in caviar, but if it is not to your liking, there are a host of other Russian specialties on the menu, and a good wine list.

✉ Ostrom utca 19, Budapest | ☎ 201 6737 🕐 Lunch, dinner

Café Pierrot (€€)

Serves Hungarian specialties with an international flavour and an extensive vegetarian menu. Piano music in the evenings.

✉ Fortuna ucta 14, Budapest | ☎ 375 6971 🕐 Lunch, dinner

Carne di Hall (€€)

Carnivores will love this cellar restaurant near the Danube. Its menu is almost exclusively devoted to meat, with steak getting special attention. The service is formal, and the wine list is a creative blend of Hungary's best and French and Italian classics.

✉ Bem rakpart 20, Budapest | ☎ 201 8137 🕐 Lunch, dinner

Dominican Restaurant (€€)

This is the restaurant of the Hilton Hotel, whose setting in the picturesque Buda Castle District makes it an attractive place to eat if you are in the area.

✉ Hess András tér 1–3, Budapest 1 ☎ 889 6757 🕐 Lunch, dinner

Firkász (€€)

Firkász exudes its journalistic background through its décor –
newspaper articles plaster walls, typewriters and cameras hang
from hooks, and photos adorn any remaining space. Its Hungarian
cuisine is top rate and the wine list features Hungary's best labels.

✉ Tátra utca 18, Budapest XIII ☎ 450 1118 🕐 Lunch, dinner

Kasca (€€)

Duck is the speciality, but the restaurant also serves other dishes.
Live piano/violin music in the evenings.

✉ Fő utca 75, Budapest I ☎ 201 9992 🕐 Lunch, dinner

Kéhli (€€)

This authentic Hungarian restaurant caters for a mainly local
clientele. It can be busy and you'll need to reserve if you prefer a
table in the main dining area, which features a gypsy band.

✉ Mókus utca 22, Budapest III ☎ 250 4241/368 0613 🕐 Lunch, dinner

Kisbuda Gyöngye (€€)

The restaurant is typically Hungarian, magnificently styled in early
20th-century bourgeois affectation, with a langurous but genial
piano-violin duo setting the mood. The place is atmospheric with a
rich and varied menu.

✉ Kenyeres út 34, Budapest III ☎ 368 6402 🕐 Mon–Sat lunch, dinner

Le Jardin de Paris (€€)

Jardin offers a few token Hungarian dishes, but why bother when
excellent French options such as trout with almond sauce and
tarragon braised rabbit leg fill the menu. The interior is simple yet
stylish, with white-washed walls and stained-glass windows.

✉ Fő utca 20, Budapest I ☎ 201 0047 🕐 Lunch, dinner

Leroy Cafe (€€)

This is hugely popular with office workers for its quick service,
large menu, and daily specials. Everything from Indonesian
chicken curry to Italian pastas is available.

✉ Bécsi ut 63, Budapest III ☎ 439 1698 🕐 Lunch, dinner

Maharaja (€)
Maharaja serves the most authentic Indian cuisine in these parts. Certainly, it's toned down for Hungarian palates, but its rogan josh or korma have enough spice to please all the same.
✉ Bécsi ut 89-91, Budapest III ☎ 250 7544 🕔 Lunch, dinner

Maligán (€€–€€€)
Serene cellar surroundings and extravagant modern Hungarian cuisine make Maligán an exemplary Óbuda restaurant, but it's the wine that lifts this restaurant into stellar orbit.
✉ Lagos utca 38, Budapest III ☎ 240 9010 🕔 Lunch, dinner

Malomtó (€€–€€€)
Malomtó scores high for its location and food. Choose from a range of imaginative international options and enjoy the flavours while relaxing next to the adjacent small lake. Once you've finished, scoot around the lake and take a peek at the Turkish bathhouse ruins, complete with cupola and pool.
✉ Frankel Leó ut 48, Budapest II ☎ 336 1830 🕔 Lunch, dinner

Mennyei Ízek (€)
This small, simple establishment almost opposite the military amphitheatre has surprisingly good Korean and Chinese cuisine. It's more of a take-away place, so order the lunch special (soup or spring roll plus main dish) and take a Roman pew across the road.
✉ Pacsiritamező utca 13, Budapest III ☎ 388 6430 🕔 Lunch

Rivalda (€€€)
The restaurant has a theatrically inspired décor, hence the name (Front of Stage). The Castle Theatre is next door. Pleasant jazz piano music in the evenings.
✉ Szinház utca 5–9, Budapest I ☎ 489 0236 🕔 Lunch, dinner

Seoul House (€)
A Korean restaurant, Seoul House serves authentic *kimchee*, and excellent beef dishes in a very pleasant and friendly atmosphere.
✉ Fő utca 8, Budapest I ☎ 201 7452 🕔 Lunch, dinner. Closed Sun

Szent Jupát (€)

This highly recommended restaurant serves mainly Hungarian dishes from an extensive menu. The huge portions are excellently prepared and cooked, and there is a good selection of beers and wines. Be prepared to share a table; here you'll find a genial atmosphere and busy staff.

✉ Retek utca 16, Budapest II ☎ 212 2923 ◷ Lunch, dinner

Új Sipos Halászkert (€€)

The restaurant, in the picturesque main square of Old Buda, specializes in a wide selection of river fish from Hungarian lakes and rivers, as well as other Hungarian dishes.

✉ Fő tér 6, Budapest III ☎ 388 8745 ◷ Lunch, dinner

Vadrózsa (€€€)

Excellent food is served in a small baroque villa also offering open-air dining in a pleasant garden. Specialties include grilled goose liver and a variety of game dishes. Piano music is played.

✉ Pentelei Molnár utca 15, Budapest II ☎ 326 5817 ◷ Lunch, dinner

CAFÉS

Angelika

Housed in the vaulted rectory of Szent Anna templom (► 93), Angelika is a suitably respectable café that attracts an older clientele happy to sit and chat the day away.

✉ Batthyány tér 7, Budapest I ☎ 212 3784

Daubner

Daubner has constant queues of eager sweet-toothers waiting for its delectable cakes and pastries despite its poor location far from much of anything. Unfortunately there's nowhere to sit though.

✉ Szépvölgyi út 50, Budapest II ☎ 335 2253

Miró

Attracting a young crowd, the café is designed entirely in the spirit of the Catalan artist whose name it celebrates.

✉ Úri utca 30, Budapest I ☎ 201 4473

Ruszwurm
Claims to be the city's oldest existing café; in the Castle District.
Excellent cakes can be eaten here or taken away.

✉ Szentháromság utca, Budapest I ☎ 375 5284

SHOPPING

Koller
Works by sculptors and painters such as Imre Varga. Worth a visit
if only to browse the lovely exhibits.

✉ Táncsics Mihály út 5, Budapest 1 ☎ 356 9208

Herendi Majolika
Herend 'village pottery' and Ajika crystal ranging from table
services to individual pieces.

✉ Bem rakpart, Budapest I ☎ 356 7899 ⏱ Tue–Fri–5, Sat 9–12

Budapest Bortársaság (Wine Society)
A fine selection of over 100 wines from Hungarian vintners, with
free tasting on Saturdays.

✉ Batthyány tér 59, Budapest I ☎ 212 0262

Demi John
Owned by the famous Interconsult Winery Neszmely, this outlet
specializes in its own outstanding wines.

✉ Margit utca 29, Budapest II ☎ 326 4984

Herend
The celebrated porcelain makers Herend sell their beautiful and
elaborate wares close to the centre of Castle Hill.

✉ Szentháromság utca 5, Budapest I ☎ 225 1050

Mammut
One of the city's largest shopping malls, it houses High Street
names and smaller specialist shops, such as Tobacconist (☎ 345
8535), which stocks a huge array of cigars, and Budai Borvár
(☎ 345 8098), whose wine selection is well above par.

✉ Lövőház utca, Budapest II ☎ 345 8020

Relikvia

One of the few antiques shops inside the castle walls (in the Hilton).

✉ Fortuna utca 21, Budapest I | ☎ 356 9973

The House of Hungarian Wines

The richest selection of Hungarian wines to buy and taste in a real cellar. It is opposite the Hilton Hotel in the Castle District.

✉ Szentháromság tér 6, Budapest I | ☎ 212 1031

Trapper Farmer

Those looking for retro jeans and shirts from the communist era (but newly made) should head here.

✉ Fő utca 92, Budapest II | ☎ 201 7961

ENTERTAINMENT

NIGHTLIFE

Bambi

Bambi's interior design is authentically communist, with many of the original 60s fittings still in place. A gem.

✉ Frankel Leó út 2-4, Budapest I | ☎ 212 3171

Lánchíd Söröző

A small and inviting pub in Víziváros with a retro look.

✉ Fő utca 4, Budapest I | ☎ 214 3144

LIVE ARTS

International Buda Stage

In the Buda Hills, this small theatre stages both English- and Hungarian-language plays, along with films, concerts and dance.

✉ Tárogató út 2-4, Budapest II | ☎ 391 2525

Nemzeti Várszínház (National Dance Theatre)

On Castle Hill, the National Dance Theatre is the best place to catch dance in the country. Performances range from classic ballets to experimental gypsy works.

✉ Színház utca 1–3, Budapest I | ☎ 201 4407; www.dancetheatre.hu

Óbudai Társaskör (Óbuda Society)

This small venue in the heart of Óbuda hosts a variety of performances, from orchestral pieces to Hungarian folk concerts.

✉ Kiskorona utca 7, Budapest III ☎ 250 0288

CHILDREN'S ENTERTAINMENT

Budavári Labirintus (Budavár Labyrinth)

See page 77.

Hadtörténeti Múzeum (Museum of Military History)

See page 82.

Uránia Csillagvizsgáló (Urania Observatory)

✉ Sánc ucta 3/B, Budapest I ☎ 386 9233 🕐 Mon–Fri 6–10 in clear weather 🚌 27

Gyermek Vasút (Children's Railway)

See page 62.

Libegő (Chairlift)

See page 63.

Sikló (Funicular)

See page 84.

SPORT

Bowling

An increasingly popular pastime in Budapest which can be pursued in one of Budapest's largest shopping malls, Mammut.

Mammut Bowling Club

✉ Lövőház utca 2–6, Budapest II ☎ 345 8300

Horse-riding

Hungarians have a tradition of horsemanship and two places worth considering for riding are Budapest Equestrian Club and Petneházy Horse-riding School.

✉ Feketefej ut 2–4, Budapest II ☎ 313 5210

Gellért-hegy and the Tabán

Towering over the Danube at a height of 230m (754ft), Gellért Hill is hard to miss. Topped with an impressive monument, it makes a magnet for tourists. The Tabán on the other hand attracts few visitors, but is a unique corner of the city that is worth exploring.

Visitors to lofty Gellért-hegy will find expansive views of the city, a forbidding 19th-century Citadella, atmospheric Sziklatemplom (cave church) and a stunning art nouveau thermal bath, the Gellért Gyógyfürdő (Gellért Thermal Baths).

The Taban, a small valley squeezed between Gellért-hegy and Vár-hegy is today a peaceful, leafy place that was once home to a large portion of Budapest's 18th- and 19th-century Serbian population. Only a few buildings remain from this time, including the Rác Gyógyfürdő (Rác thermal baths ➤ 67). Here also is the statue of the beloved Empress Elizabeth, the quintessential 'It girl' of the 19th century.

Gellért-hegy
Best places to see, ➤ 38–39.

CITADELLA (CITADEL)
This grim, formidable stronghold on top of Gellért-hegy (Gellért Hill) was built after the Revolution of 1848–49, its principal military purpose to control Castle Hill. Parts of it were symbolically demolished in 1894. In the past it had several functions, as a prison camp, temporary accommodation for the homeless, the site of an anti-aircraft battery, and, more recently, a tourist attraction. Since it's a unique viewing point from which to look down on the city (telescope rental available), it is worth the walk. At the eastern end of the citadel is the Liberation Monument (➤ 109).

🚇 3L 🖂 Citadella sétány, Budapest XI ☎ 365 6076
🍴 Café (€€) ⏰ Open access 🚌 Bus: 27; tram: 18, 19, 47, 49 ❓ A magnificent fireworks display takes place on Géllert Hill on 20 Aug

GELLÉRT EMLÉKMŰ (GELLÉRT MONUMENT)
Facing the Buda end of Elizabeth Bridge, the monument was erected in 1904, and is one of the ten royal statues donated to the capital by Emperor Franz Joseph. Impressive though it is – especially at night when floodlit – its story is more interesting. It was from the top of Gellért Hill, where the monument stands, that St Gellért (Gerard), the Bishop of Csanád, was pushed by pagan Hungarians he had come to convert to Christianity. After this ignominious fall, legend tells that he was nailed up in a barrel and thrown unceremoniously into the Danube.

🚇 4K 🖂 Gellért-hegy, Budapest XI ⏰ Open access 🎟 Free 🍴 Panorama Restaurant (€€) 🚌 Bus: 27; tram: 18, 19

HOTEL GELLÉRT ÉS GELLÉRT GYÓGYFÜRDŐ
(GELLÉRT HOTEL AND GELLÉRT THERMAL BATHS)

Described by a local illustrator as a 'huge white gem', the Danubius Gellért Hotel (to give it its full name) is one of the most prestigious in Budapest. The hotel, together with its thermal baths, was built as part of a major civic policy to make Budapest into a city of baths. If not taking a dip, then have a look at the mosaic floor and glass ceiling. From the back of the hall

you can see into the roofed part of the swimming pool. Also see the outdoor pool, which was recently enlarged, its polished postmodern lines contrasting with the bulky art nouveau building which was completed in 1918. The outdoor pool stretches to the other side of Kemenes utca and is connected to the main area by a subway. But if you're not feeling energetic, you can relax with an ice-cream or a beer on the terrace.

🚹 4M ✉ Hotel: Szent Gellért tér 1, Budapest XI. Thermal baths: Kelenhegyi út 2–4, Budapest XI ☎ Hotel: 889 5500. Thermal baths: 466 6166
🍴 Panorama Restaurant (€€) 🚌 Bus: 7, 7a, 86; tram: 18, 19, 47, 49
✋ Hotel: free. Baths: free if a resident of the hotel, otherwise expensive

SZABADSÁG HÍD (FREEDOM BRIDGE)

This masterpiece of aesthetic engineering was opened in 1896 as part of the millennium celebrations, when Emperor Franz Joseph himself hammered in the final rivet. 'When designing the bridge,' said its architect, Virgil Nagy, 'I had to obey the requirements of

beauty, simplicity and economy'. On top of each pillar, surmounting a golden ball, is a Turul, Hungary's mythical bird.

➕ 5L ✉ Szent Gellért tér, Budapest XI to Fővám tér, Budapest VI
🍴 Panorama Restaurant (€€) 🚌 Bus: 86, 7, 7a; tram: 47, 49, 18, 19;

SZABADSÁG SZOBOR (LIBERATION MONUMENT)

Situated by the Citadella as a sombre reminder of Budapest's more recent turbulent past, the Liberation, or Freedom, Monument commemorates the Soviet-led liberation of the city from the Germans in 1945. Originally intended to honour the dictator Admiral Horthy's son (a young pilot who died in a crash believed to have been egineered by the Germans), the monument was adapted by the Communists to reflect a new era, with the addition of a soldier figure and the inscription: 'To the liberating Soviet heroes from a grateful Hungarian people'. However, few Hungarians who lived through that time shared the sentiment, and the monument has been adapted again with the removal of the soldier.

➕ 4L ✉ Citadella sétány, Budapest XI ☎ 175 6451 🕐 Open access
✋ Free 🍴 Aranyszarvas (€€) 🚌 Bus: 27; tram: 18, 19

SZIKLATEMPLOM (CAVE CHURCH)

The unusual Sziklatemplom overlooks the Danube opposite Gellért Hotel on the hill's southern side. Built by the Pauline order in 1931, it was closed in the early 50s by the communists who immediately bordered up the entranceway and jailed the monks. It reopened in 1990 and has been in use since 1992. The interior is warm and comfortable, with tiled flooring, plants, stained-glass windows and natural cave walls; religious ornaments are surprisingly few. Note the slab of concrete to the right of the church entrance as you enter – it's the last remnant of the wall that once closed in the church.

➕ 4L ✉ Gellért-hegy, Budapest XI ☎ 385 1529 🕐 9–9 ✋ Free
🍴 Panorama Restaurant (€€) 🚌 Tram: 19, 47, 49

The Tabán

ERZSÉBET KIRÁLYNÉ SZOBOR
(STATUE OF QUEEN ELISABETH)

This statue honours Elisabeth (1837–98), wife of Habsburg
Emperor Franz Joseph. Descended from Bavarian aristocrats, the
beautiful Elisabeth (or 'Sissi' as she was fondly known), was one
of the few members of the ruling dynasty to win the affections of
Hungarians. Estranged from her husband, Sissi met an untimely
end at the hands of an assassin on the banks of Lake Geneva. The
nation went into deep mourning at the news of her death.

✚ 4K ✉ Döbrentei tér, Budapest I 🚋 Tram: 18, 19

RUDAS GYÓGYFÜRDŐ (RUDAS THERMAL BATHS)

The first thermal baths built on the site of Rudas date from the
14th century, but the current incarnation, which has had a
thorough renovation, was constructed by the Turks in 1566. It is
arguably the most Turkish of all Budapest's baths, and a soak in its
domed octagonal room, particularly when the sun pierces the
roof's small windows, is not only a soothing experience but also a

trip back in time. The Turkish baths are
men only Monday to Friday, except on
Tuesday which it's women only; on
weekends it's mixed but swimwear is
required. The swimming pool wing,
dating from the first half of the 1800s,
is neoclassical in style and has mixed
bathing throughout the week.

✚ 4K ✉ Döbrentei tér 9, Budapest I
☎ 356 1322 🕐 Swimming pools: Mon–Fri
6–6, Sat, Sun 8–5. Baths: Mon–Thu 6–8,
Fri 6am–8pm, 10–4, Sat 8–5, 10–4, Sun 8–5
✋ Swimming pools: moderate; thermal
baths: expensive 🚌 Bus: 7; tram: 18, 19;

SEMMELWEIS ORVOSTÖRTÉNETI MÚZEUM (MUSEUM OF MEDICAL HISTORY)

Semmelweis is one of the more intriguing yet overlooked museums in the city. It documents the history of medicine from early tribal practices to the beginning of the 20th century through a vast array of highly unusual artefacts, including a mummified human head and falcon from Egypt. Wax models of various human organs are incredibly detailed, while the tools of surgery from the 16th- to 19th-centuries look particularly nasty. One room contains the reconstructed Holy Ghost Pharmacy, founded in 1786, while another contains a 19th-century dentist's chair which would be perfect for a good horror flick.

The museum is named after Ignác Semmelweis, the doctor who discovered the cause of peurperal fever. Known as the 'saviour of mothers', he realized doctors needed to sterilize their hands, clothes and instruments between autopsies and assisting with births. He was born in the house and is buried in its quiet garden.

✚ 3K ✉ Apród utca 1–3, Budapest I ☎ 201 1577 🕐 Mid-Mar to Oct Tue–Sun 10:30–5:30; Nov to mid-Mar Tue–Sun 10:30–4:30
✋ Inexpensive 🚋 Tram: 19

SZARVAS-HÁZ (DEER HOUSE)

This triangular-shaped café was built at the beginning of the 19th century in late rococo style. Famous for its game dishes, it's now the Aranyszarvas Restaurant. The Deer House was once part of the Tában, a popular place of entertainment on the northern slope of Gellért Hill. Many of the houses here, apart from the Deer House, were demolished for public health reasons. All the more reason to eat at the Deer House, which is scrupulously clean.

✚ 3K ✉ Szarvas tér, Budapest I ☎ 375 6451 🕐 Daily noon–11
✋ Free 🍴 Aranyszarvas (€€) 🚌 Bus: 16, 78; tram: 19

HOTELS

Ábel Panzió (€)

This small but comfortable place, in a quiet area just southwest of the Citadel, has ten rooms, all with bathrooms and phones.

✉ Ábel Jenő utca 9, Budapest XI ☎ 209 2537

Danubius Hotel Flamenco (€€€)

This is a large and modern hotel, just south of Gellért Hill a few minutes from the business and shopping areas. With 348 rooms, including ten suites, it offers a wide range of facilities: restaurant, bars, live music, car rental, a business centre and full leisure facilities.

✉ Tas vezér utca 3–7, Budapest XI ☎ 889 5600; www.danubiusgroup.com

Danubius Hotel Gellért (€€)

This traditional *fin de siècle* spa hotel with a magnificent pool has a mosaic floor and glass ceiling. A comfortable, four-star hotel with 239 rooms, it is blissfully indifferent to the demands of modern life. The splendid restaurant has river views.

✉ Szent Gellért tér 1, Budapest XI ☎ 889 5500; www.danubiusgroup.com

Hotel Citadella (€)

As its name suggests, this small and basic 15-room hotel, which has seen better days, is near the Citadel on top of Gellért Hill. It has a restaurant, brasserie and private parking.

✉ Citadella sétány, Budapest XI ☎ 466 5794

RESTAURANTS

Aranyszarvas (€€)

Located in the Deer House (► 112), Aranyszarvas is a well-established restaurant that's been serving guests for many years. Its solid Hungarian menu follows the seasons, although game, the restaurant's forte, is ever-present – choices include wild boar, stag, venison, pheasant and hare.

✉ Szarvas tér 1, Budapest I ☎ 375 6451 🕓 Lunch, dinner

Panorama Restaurant (€€)

The famous Gellért Hotel's restaurant offers views of the Danube that are as appetizing as the food. Pikeperch dishes and veal Gellért-style are among the many house specialties on the menu.

🖾 Gellért tér 1, Budapest XI ☎ 889 5550 🕔 Lunch, dinner

Szeged Vendéglő (€)

This is a traditional Hungarian restaurant next to the Gellért Hotel specializing in fish dishes, and also Hungarian and French cuisine. Another feature is live gypsy music and a folk programme.

🖾 Bartók Béla út 1, Budapest XI ☎ 209 1668 🕔 Lunch, dinner

Tabáni Terasz (€€)

The tastefully renovated 250-year-old house and protected inner courtyard are reasons enough to dine at Tabáni. The international menu features some delectable dishes, including a smattering of Southeast Asian choices. Fish is a specialty.

🖾 Apród utca 10, Budapest I ☎ 201 108 🕔 Lunch, dinner

ENTERTAINMENT

A38

Moored by the Buda end of Petőfi Bridge, this Ukranian cargo boat has been transformed into a hip venue, with dancing, concerts, bars and a restaurant.

🖾 Mıegyetem rakpart, Budapest XI ☎ 464 3940

Fonó Budai Zeneház (Fonó Buda Music House)

Fonó is the centre of Hungarian folk and world music in Budapest. Its full programme features traditional bands at 8pm every Wednesday and Friday night, and Saturday is often graced with bigger, international acts.

🖾 Sztregova utca 3, Budapest XI ☎ 206 5300; www.fono.hu

Belváros and Lipótváros

For centuries Belváros *was* Pest – nothing existed outside its medieval walls. Nowadays it is the heart of Budapest on the east side of the Danube and filled with exclusive boutiques and gorgeous art nouveau architecture. But some of the city's most celebrated architecture can also be found in Lipótváros, the business centre which occupies the northern half of the fifth district.

Stretching through Belvaros is the pedestrian boulevard Váci utca, alive with tourists searching for holiday gifts or tailor-made outfits. Further north in Lipotvaros, you'll find enormous squares and some exceptional examples of Budapest's celebrated architectural styles, including the neoclassical Országház (Parliament ➤ 48) and Szent István Bazilika (St Stephen's Basilica ➤ 50), and the art nouveau Gresham Palace (➤ 122) and Magyar Királyi Takarék Pénztár (Former Royal Post Office Savings Bank ➤ 123).

Belváros

BELVÁROSI PLÉBÁNIA TEMPLOM (INNER CITY PARISH CHURCH)

This beautiful church is one of the oldest in the city and is situated uncomfortably close to Elizabeth Bridge on Március 15 tér. The area was once the centre of the 4th-century Roman settlement of *Contra-Aquincum* and a small display of its remains can be seen close by. Dating from the 12th century, the church was rebuilt in the 18th century after a devastating fire, hence the baroque façade and

interior. At one time the Turks converted it into a mosque and you can still see a Muslim prayer niche or *mihrab* to the right of the high altar. If you can bear the flyover with all its traffic, delight in the beauty of this church and curse the city planners.

🕂 4K ✉ Március 15 tér, Budapest V ☎ 318 3108 🕔 Mon–Sat 9–12:30, 6–7, Sun 6:30am–7:30am, 6pm–7pm 🎫 Free Ⓜ M3 Ferenciek tér 🚋 Tram: 2

DUNAKORZÓ (DANUBE PROMENADE)

In the latter years of the 19th century much of neoclassical Pest was hidden by large hotels, some the finest and most fashionable in Europe – the Carlton, Ritz, Hungaria and the Bristol. This is where the rich and fashionable strolled during the summer months, a tradition that had survived from the time when Pest was a small town. It was especially beautiful in the evening with brightly lit cafés and jazz and gypsy music. Now with new hotels in the area, the promenade has come to life again, not least because of its magnificent view across the great river to Castle Hill.

🕂 4J ✉ Vigadó tér, Budapest V 🍴 Gerbeaud (€€) 🚋 Tram: 2

FÖLDALATTI VASÚTI MÚZEUM
(UNDERGROUND RAILWAY MUSEUM)

Hidden away in the metro station underpass on Deák tér, this tiny, exquisite museum occupies one of the original railway tunnels. Its exhibition includes a fascinating array of plans, models and carriages, and shows the development of the first underground system on the European mainland. The first line, completed in 1896, ran the entire length of Andrássy út, a distance of 3.5km (5.6 miles). The museum is definitely worth a visit if you're an eager trainspotter. Even if you're not exactly a train fanatic, it's something to keep in mind for a rainy day.

✚ 5J ⊠ Deák tér, Budapest V ☎ 461 6500 🕓 Apr–Oct Tue–Sun 10–5; Nov–Mar Tue–Sun 10–4 💵 Inexpensive 🚇 M1/2/3 Deák tér 🚌 Bus: 9, 16, 105; tram: 47, 49

MAGYAR KERESKEDELMI ÉS VENDÉGLÁTÓIPARI MÚZEUM
(HUNGARIAN MUSEUM OF TOURISM AND TRADE)

Hungary's museum of tourism and trade is a unique beast, focusing its attention – strangely, considering its name – on the world of catering and commerce. Its commerce section has displays of store signs, promotional material, product packaging, and even invoices and accounting books, but most visitors will find the catering wing far more engaging. Here, the large collection of cooking utensils and moulds will make most amateur chefs weep, and the plethora of restaurant menus is impressive. The reconstructed 19th-century cake shop is also a must for any dessert-lover

✚ 5H ⊠ Szent István tér 15, Budapest V ☎ 375 6249 🕓 Wed–Mon 11–7 💵 Moderate 🍴 Café Kör (€€) 🚇 M2 Arany János utca

VÖRÖSMARTY TÉR (SQUARE) AND VÁCI UTCA (STREET)

Named after the 19th-century Romantic poet Mihály Vörösmarty (1800–55), the square is a real delight. The poet's monument stands in the centre. On the north side, at No 7, is the famous Gerbeaud pastry shop – just the place for a tasty snack. Váci utca, on the far side of the square, is Budapest's premier shopping street. The shopping here is small scale with big brand names – Estée Lauder, Adidas and the like. The entire street is pedestrianized but, attractive as it is, it looks much like any European pedestrianized shopping area.

🕂 4J 🖂 Budapest V 🍴 Resti (€) 🚇 M1 Vörösmarty tér 🚌 Tram: 2

a walk in the Inner City

This walk in downtown Pest serves as an introduction to the commercial and cultural heart of the city.

Start at Kossuth Lajos tér outside the magnificent Parliament (▶ 48). With your back to the Parliament, turn right down Nádor utca towards Szabadság tér, a hidden gem of the city.

At Nos 8–9 is the stately bulk of the Hungarian National Bank. On the southwest corner towards the square is the figure of Hamlet holding poor Yorick's skull.

Return to Nádor utca and turn right towards József Attila utca. Before reaching it, turn right into Roosevelt tér.

At the northern end is the Hungarian Academy of Sciences (▶ 123), the first neo-Renaissance building in the city, built between 1862 and 1864. Also on the square is Gresham Palace (▶ 122), a richly ornate art nouveau building.

Back on Nádor utca, turn right. You come to the intersection with József Attila utca, with its incessant flow of traffic. Cross it and head straight on to József nádor tér, which, before the advent of the automobile, was one of the most attractive squares in the city.

Occupying the square is the Romantic-style Postabank Headquarters; Gross House, a neoclassical apartment buildings; and the Central European University, a classical chef-d'oeuvre.

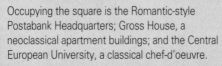

Leave József nádor tér and make for Bécsi utca. Turn right, and walk down to Vörösmarty tér, a pleasant and restful square.

At No 7 is the famous Gerbeaud pastry shop – so stop for a snack.

Walk to the far side to Váci utca (▶ 119), the most stylish shopping street in town. If you can resist the shops, continue under the subway towards the Central Market Hall on Vámház körút.

The 19th-century market hall (▶ 165) is a place to wander or have a snack or beer at one of the small upstairs bars.

Distance Approximately 3km (2 miles)
Time 2 hours, half a day with stops
Start point Kossuth Lajos tér ✚ 4F ◉ M2 Kossuth Lajos tér
End point Central Market Hall (Vásárcsarnok) ✚ 5L
◉ Tram: 2, 2/A, 47, 49; trolley bus: 83
Lunch Fatál (€) ✉ Váci utca 67 266 2607

Lipótváros

GRESHAM PALACE

Gresham Palace began life as a luxury apartment building/office space of the London-based Gresham Life Insurance Company in 1906. The company commissioned Zsigmond Quittner to deliver the goods, who in turn hired builders József and László Vágó. The open purse and artistic freedom afforded by Gresham allowed Quittner to create a lavish art nouveau design and install the latest technological advances, such as central heating and a dust extraction system. By the end of World War II however the palace was in a sorry state, its façade scarred by bomb blasts and its interior ruined by Soviet soldiers. During the communist era the palace was converted into cheap apartments and shops, but in

1998 developers bought the dilapidated building with the intention of turning the historical landmark into a luxury hotel (Four Seasons Hotel ➤ 126). After a $US110 million makeover, the Gresham is once again the pride of Budapest. The T-shaped arcade is restored as a resplendent work of art, topped by a glazed roof, floored with tiled mosaics, and walled with colourful Zsolnay ceramics. The original wrought-iron gate, with its flamboyant peacock motifs, marks the entrance, and a stained-glass window by Miksa Róth featuring Lajos Kossuth complements the second-floor staircase.

➕ 4H ✉ Roosevelt tér 5–6, Budapest V ☎ 268 6000 🍴 Gresham Café (€)
🚌 Tram: 2

MAGYAR KIRÁLYI POSTA TAKARÉK PENZTÁR (FORMER ROYAL POST OFFICE SAVINGS BANK)

Designed by Ödön Lechner in 1900, the Post Office Savings Bank is an exceptional example of Hungarian art nouveau that still manages to impress more than a hundred years later. The façade is a fantastical mix of secessionist styles and Hungarian folk art motifs – look for the swarms of bees climbing the walls to beehives, representative of thrift and saving. The majesty of the lime-green roof is hard to see from street level, but what can be seen of its vibrant Zsolany tiles and flourishes of yellow trimming is truly captivating. Unfortunately the interior is closed to the public (the building now belongs to the National Bank) and can only be visited one day in May – phone for details. It is however possible to take a peek at the Cashiers' Hall during normal working hours.

➕ 4G ✉ Hold utca 4 ☎ 428 2600 🍴 Farger Kávé (€)
🚇 M3 Arany János utca

MAGYAR TUDOMÁNYOS AKADÉMIA (HUNGARIAN ACADEMY OF SCIENCES)

This austere neo-Renaissance building on the northern side of Roosevelt tér was built in 1865 by Friedrich Stuler to house Hungary's Academy of Sciences. The academy was founded 40

years earlier by Count István Széchenyi, who gifted one year's income for the establishment of an institution to explore Hungarian science, arts, literature and language. The act is captured in a bronze relief facing Akadémia utca. Statues of seminal figures from various fields of science also grace the building's façade: look for Newton, Lomonosov, Galilei, Révay, Descartes and Leibnitz. The academy shares Roosevelt tér with the Gresham Palace, a statue of Széchenyi, and another of Ferenc Deák.

✚ 4H ✉ Roosevelt tér, Budapest V 🍽 Lou Lou (€€) 🚃 Tram: 2

NÉPRAJZI MÚZEUM (MUSEUM OF ETHNOGRAPHY)

Strongly resembling Berlin's Reichstag, but much more elegant, this neo-Renaissance palace was built to house the Supreme Court and the Chief Public Prosecutor's Office. Sculptures of legislators, magistrates and goddesses of justice adorn the façade of this large and imposing building. Its grandiose entrance hall features a marble stairway, huge chandeliers and on the ceiling a splendid fresco by Karoly Lotz. Again, this is worth visiting if only for its magnificent architecture and décor. Permanent exhibitions include ethnological material from across Hungary, including traditional folk costumes, simple farming implements and household items with touches of folk design, painted pottery and furniture, and a reconstructed church from the 18th century.

🚼 4F 🖂 Kossuth Lajos tér 12, Budapest V ☎ 473 2439

🕐 Tue–Sun 10–6 🖐 Free 🍴 Café (€) 🚇 M2 Kossuth Lajos tér 🚌 Bus: 15; tram: 2; trolley bus: 70, 78

ORSZÁGHÁZ (PARLIAMENT)

Best places to see, ➤ 48–49.

SZABADSÁG TÉR (LIBERTY SQUARE)

This vast open space in the city centre between the Parliament building and St Stephen's Basilica was laid out by Antal Paloczy in 1902. The site was once occupied by a huge military barracks and prison where many a Hungarian patriot was incarcerated. Among the different palaces, one art nouveau building, the American Embassy, is very prominent. The statue in front of the building is of the US General, Harry Hill Bandholtz. An officer of the Allied peace-keeping force in 1919, he saved the treasures of the National Museum by sealing its doors. The seals bore the US coat of arms and so deterred the soldiers of the occupying Romanian army from plundering the museum. Also on the square and nearby are the headquarters of Hungarian television, the Ministry of Agriculture, the Ethnographical Museum, and the Post Office Savings Bank.

🚼 4G 🖂 Budapest V 🍴 Farger Kávé (€) 🚇 M2 Kossuth Lajos tér

🚌 Tram: 2; bus: 15

SZENT ISTVÁN BAZILIKA (ST STEPHEN'S BASILICA)

Best places to see, ➤ 50–51.

HOTELS

Astoria (€€)

Sumptuously splendid with a *fin de siècle* atmosphere, but there is nothing remotely stuffy about this pleasant three-star hotel with 130 rooms; it is relaxing and unhurried.

✉ Kossuth Lajos utca 19–21, Budapest V ☎ 889 6000; www.danubiusgroup.com

City Hotel Mátyás (€)

One of Pest's central, good value options. Rooms are fairly unexciting, but they're more than adequate.

✉ Március 15. tér 7–8, Budapest V ☎ 338 4711; www.cityhotelmatyas.hu

Four Seasons Hotel (€€€)

One of the city's landmark buildings, the magnificent art nouveau Gresham Palace dominates Roosevelt Square at the Pest end of the Chain Bridge. Immaculately restored, since 2004 it has been occupied by the five-star establishment that is surely destined to become Budapest's top hotel.

✉ 5–6 Roosevelt tér, Budapest V ☎ 268 6000; www.fourseasons.com

Hotel Art (€€)

In a side street in the heart of Old Pest, this 320-room hotel has won awards for its fresh and original architecture. Comfortable modern rooms and restaurant with Transylvanian specialities.

✉ Király Pál utca 12, Budapest V ☎ 266 2166; www.bestwestern-ce.com

Hotel Hold (€€)

Well-placed between Parliament and St Stephen's Basilica, this is a charming old hotel built around a courtyard. The intimate vaulted restaurant serves Hungarian specialities

✉ Hold utca 5, Budapest V ☎ 472 0480; www.hotelhold.hu

Kempinski Hotel Corvinus (€€€)

This striking, postmodern hotel has three elegant façades and one plain. It's 368 rooms/suites include two presidential apartments

✉ Erzsébet tér 7–8, Budapest V ☎ 429 3777; www.kempinski-budapest.com

Leo Panzió (€)

With Váci utca only one block from its front door, Leo is about as central as it gets. Rooms have a dated look but they're quite comfortable and fitted with air-conditioning for summer days.

✉ Kossuth Lajos utca 2/A, Budapest V ☎ 266 9041; www.leopanzio.hu

Le Meridien Budapest (€€€)

In an elegant building, which is a declared historic monument, this luxurious hotel has 218 rooms decorated with period furniture and chandeliers. A beautiful atrium, with a stained-glass dome, is the setting for Le Bourbon restaurant. The hotel is close to the main business and shopping districts and the main sights.

✉ Erzsébet tér 9–10, Budapest V ☎ 429 5500;
www.lemeridien-budapest.com

Sofitel Atrium Budapest (€€€)

This international hotel and conference centre with 352 rooms (including 54 suites) is suave, efficient, comfortable and has all the modern conveniences you would expect to find in a top-class hotel. You can order an official replica of any of the paintings in the National Gallery. They have it painted for you and it comes issued with a certificate as well.

✉ Roosevelt tér 2, Budapest V ☎ 266 1234; www.sofitel.com

Starlight Suiten (€€€)

'Modern' is the keystone of the Starlight Suiten. Its suites are thoroughly contemporary, featuring leather chairs and couches, carpeted floors, and gleaming, tiled bathrooms. Service is prompt and professional, and, with its location in the heart of Belváros, it's hard to find a more central location.

✉ Mérleg utca 6, Budapest V ☎ 484 3700; www.starlighthotels.com

Taverna (€€)

On Budapest's fashionable shopping street, the Taverna is a very functional concrete-and-glass four-star hotel – part of an entertainment complex – with 227 rooms and all modern facilities.

✉ Váci utca 20, Budapest V ☎ 485 3100; www.hoteltaverna.hu

RESTAURANTS

Astoria Empire (€€)
This very plush restaurant is in the impressive Astoria Hotel.
Elegant surroundings complement the high standards of
Hungarian and international fare. Gypsy bands play in the evening.
✉ Kossuth Lajos utca 19–21, Budapest V ☎ 889 6000 🕐 Lunch, dinner

Café Kör (€€)
Modern Hungarian and European food served in generous portions
and fine salad plates.
✉ Sas utca 17, Budapest V ☎ 311 0053 🕐 Lunch, dinner. Closed Sun

Cyrano (€€)
With its finely designed interior, this is a favourite of the Budapest
business community. It offers a good menu with a selection of
reasonably priced wines. The restaurant prides itself (hence its
name) on being a location for the filming of *Cyrano de Bergerac*.
✉ Kristóf tér 7–8, Budapest V ☎ 266 3096 🕐 Lunch, dinner

Dionysos (€)
On Pest Quay with an interior like an Hellenic village square, this
restaurant is located in attractive surroundings and serves a good
choice of excellent Greek dishes.
✉ Belgrád rakpart 16, Budapest V ☎ 318 1222 🕐 Lunch, dinner

Fatál (€)
This traditional restaurant offers wholesome, home-style
Hungarian dishes. The portions are generous, as is the welcome.
Payment by cash only.
✉ Váci utca 67 (entrance on Pintér utca), Budapest V ☎ 266 2607
🕐 Lunch, dinner

La Fontaine (€€)
The bistro-style restaurant is conveniently located in the heart of
the town. It serves modestly priced typical French dishes, and has
a full range of wines, beers and spirits.
✉ Mérleg utca 10, Pest V, ☎ 317 3715 🕐 Lunch, dinner

Govinda (€)

Govinda serves fresh, vegetarian Indian cuisine including polenta-based dishes, vegetable rice, dahl, and soups. Its cellar location is cool in summer and warm in winter and service is very friendly.

✉ Vigyázó Ferenc utca 4, Budapest V ☎ 269 1625 🕒 Lunch, dinner. Closed Sun

Iguana Bar & Grill (€€)

The Iguana serves excellent Mexican food and margaritas in a lively Hungarian and international atmosphere.

✉ Zoltán utca 16, Budapest V ☎ 331 4352 🕒 Lunch, dinner

Kafana (€€)

Kafana specializes in Balkan dishes, such as *cevap* (fingers of lamb and veal) and *cigany vesalica* (roast pork fillet with bacon and sun-dried plums), and attracts a solid Serbian following. On Friday and Saturday evenings the restaurant transforms into a convivial bar.

✉ Sörház utca 4, Budapest V ☎ 266 2274 🕒 Lunch Mon–Fri, dinner daily

Kárpátia (€€€)

Kárpátia's richly painted vaulted ceilings and walls are reminiscent of Mátyás templom (➤ 46), as are its stained-glass windows. The menu of Hungarian and Transylvanian specialities is small but selective, and there's accompanying gypsy music most nights.

✉ Ferenc tere 7-8, Budapest V ☎ 317 3596 🕒 Lunch, dinner

Lou Lou (€€)

This French restaurant with Hungarian appeal offers a good choice of wines, beers and spirits.

✉ Vigyázó F. utca 4, Budapest V ☎ 312 4505 🕒 Lunch, dinner. Closed Sun

Óceán Bár & Grill (€€–€€€)

Serving fresh fish flown in from Scandinavia daily, Óceán is leagues ahead of most other fish restaurants in Budapest. The interior has a fresh, clean look (aquarium included of course), with big windows overlooking the river.

✉ Petőfi tér 3, Budapest V ☎ 266 1826 🕒 Lunch, dinner

Resti (€)

You cannot get nearer the city centre, though you may still not notice this place with a Communist-nostalgia décor of red stars and agitprop posters. It serves Hungarian dishes.

✉ Deák Ferenc utca 2, Budapest V ☎ 266 6210 🕙 Lunch, dinner

Spoon (€€–€€€)

Spoon is one of a string of boat-restaurants on the Danube with views of Buda, its twin hills, and the Széchenyi lanchíd (➤ 84–85). It stands out for its superb Hungarian wines and varied international menu, which also caters for vegetarians and children.

✉ Vigadó tér 3, Budapest V ☎ 411 0933 🕙 Lunch, dinner

CAFÉS

Café Alibi

A neat, unpretentious café, Alibi attracts a mainly female crowd with its quiet ambience, strong coffee and rich hot chocolate.

✉ Egyetem tér 4, Budapest V ☎ 317 4209

Central Kávéház

An archetypal turn-of-20th-century Budapest coffee house that has been lovingly restored to its original glory. You can dine or just indulge in coffee and succulent cakes.

✉ Kàroly Mihàly utca 9, Budapest V ☎ 266 2110/4572

Farger Kávé

A modern café that's hugely popular with laptop owners looking for free wireless connection over breakfast or a long, drawn-out coffee. Children are heartily welcomed and the best window seats overlooking Szabadság tér normally fill up first.

✉ Zoltán utca 18, Budapest V ☎ 373 0078

Gerbeaud

Another venerable city institution, Gerbeaud has been here since 1870. The café serves a fine selection of pastries and there is now a restaurant and beer hall with its own micro-brewery.

✉ Vörösmary tér 7, Budapest V ☎ 429 9000

Gresham Café

Gresham recalls the heady days of the 1920s when the Gresham Circle, a group of Budapest's literary elite, met here to exchange ideas and broaden minds. Its lovingly reconstructed art deco interior is a perfect complement to the rest of the palace (➤ 122).

✉ Roosevelt tér 5–6, Budapest V ☎ 268 5100

SHOPPING

ANTIQUES AND ART

Antik Millennium

True to its name, it has a wonderful array of antiques and specializes in antique linens, dresses, shawls, dolls and jewellery. A cosy place.

✉ Váci utca 67, Budapest V ☎ 318 1478

Antik Diszkont

A cash-only shop specializing in furniture and chandeliers in a variety of styles. Not really for small-item hunters.

✉ Falk Miksa utca 10, Budapest V ☎ 311 3030

Arten Gallery

A stimulating and well-exhibited selection of contemporary Hungarian artists such as Arnold Gross.

✉ Váci utca 25, Budapest V ☎ 266 3127

Bardoni

On the corner of Falk Miksa utca, this has a good selection of 20th-century furniture and other items. The emphasis here is on art deco.

✉ Markó utca 2, Budapest V ☎ 269 0090

BÁV

Bizományi Árúhaz Vállalat (BÁV), the state-owned chain, offers one of the best chances to pick up a bargain. The outlets sell paintings, jewellery, carpets, porcelain, rugs and furnishings. This is one of many branches.

✉ Bécsi utca 1–3, Budapest V ☎ 317 2548

Csók István Gallery

Certainly one of the best galleries for contemporary Hungarian art.

✉ Váci utca 25, Budapest V ☎ 318 5826

Galléria Kieselbach

The leading venue for (mostly 20th-century) Hungarian art.

✉ Szent István körút 5, Budapest V ☎ 269 3148

Haas Galéria

It's worth going up the dimly lit steps and across the gloomy courtyard to find this intimate gallery specializing in the little-known Hungarian contribution to 20th-century avant-garde art.

✉ Falk Miksa utca 6, Budapest V ☎ 332 3253

Hephaistos Háza

Wrought iron features heavily at this furniture/interior design store stocking Magyar designers.

✉ Molnár utca 27, Budapest V ☎ 266 1550

Magma

Showcases the latest Hungarian designers and their work, which ranges from porcelain to furniture.

✉ Petőfi Sándor utca 11, Budapest V ☎ 235 0277

Montparnasse

Museum-quality, mostly French, restored art deco furniture.

✉ Falk Miksa utca 17, Budapest V ☎ 951 1251

Mű-Terem Gallery

Art deco pieces and 19th- and 20th-century paintings.

✉ Falk Miksa utca 30 ☎ 312 2071

BOOKS

Bestsellers

Wide range of fiction and non-fiction, magazines, guides, dictionaries. The best English-language bookshop.

✉ Október 6 út 11, Budapest V ☎ 312 1295

Központi Antikvárium

The Central Antiquarian Bookshop, established in 1881, with a
huge selection of maps and foreign books.

✉ Múzeum körút 13–15, Budapest V ☎ 317 3514

Libri Stúdium

Good selection of foreign-language books in this central branch of
a leading chain of booksellers. Other well-stocked outlets, with
cafés, at Rákóczi út 12 and in the Mammut mall.

✉ Váci utca 22, Budapest V ☎ 318 5680

Nyugat Antikvárium

Shelves of rare foreign-language books, prints and maps that can
keep you browsing for hours.

✉ Bajcsy-Zsilinszky út 34, Budapest V ☎ 311 9023 🚇 Arany János utca

FASHION

Carum Carvi Fashion House

If you want a made-to-measure suit, try here. Also does off-the-
peg clothes, for men and women.

✉ Pest V, Kossuth Lajos utca 17 🕐 Mon–Fri 10–6, Sat 10–1

Nárry Tamás

Creates original and off-the-rack outfits for women.

✉ Károlyi Mihály utca 12, Budapest V ☎ 266 2473

Tango Classic

Attractive, wearable outfits inspired by traditional Hungarian
costumes.

✉ Váci utca 8, Budapest V ☎ 318 9741

GIFTS, JEWELLERY AND MUSIC

Folkart Centrum

Sells Hungarian-made folk art in the form of clothes, pottery, dolls,
and lace work at reasonable prices.

✉ Váci utca 58, Budapest V ☎ 318 5840

Holló Atelier
Beautiful, high-quality northeast Hungarian pottery which began manufacturing porcelain in 1954.

✉ Marriot Hotel Pergola, Apáczai Csere János utca, Budapest V ☎ 266 7000

M. Frey Wille
Head here for matching jewellery featuring Klimt and Egyptian motifs from the Vienna-based designers.

✉ Régiposta utca 19, Budapest V ☎ 318 7665

Porcelánház
As the name suggests, this folk shop specializes in porcelain and pottery, mainly from southeastern Hungary.

✉ Váci utca 45, Budapest V ☎ 266 3165

Rózsavölgyi
This is an old, established music shop specializing in classical music and sheet music. Also folk and rock sections.

✉ Szervita tér 5, Budapest V ☎ 318 3500 🕐 Mon–Fri 10–6, Sat 10–2

FOOD AND DRINK
La Boutique des Vins
This shop offers an excellent selection of Hungarian and international wines; expert advice is also on hand.

✉ Jozsef Attila utca 12, Budapest V ☎ 317 5919

Hold utcai vásárcsarnok
Near Parliament, this food hall is a compact alternative to the massive Central Market for quality farm produce and much more.

✉ Hold utca 13, Budapest V ☎ 332 3976

Számos Marcipán
If you have a sweet-tooth, you will love this store for its large and creative selection of marzipan delights.

✉ Párizsi utca 3, Budapest V ☎ 317 3643

ENTERTAINMENT

NIGHTLIFE

Beckett's

This great Irish-style pub serves good grub and beer. Frequented by homesick expats.

✉ Bajcsy–Zsilinszky ut 72, Budapest V ☎ 311 1035 ⏱ Daily 12 till late

Irish Cat Pub

This crowded but friendly bar attracts a range of visitors and locals in search of Guinness and the occasional band.

✉ Múzeum körút 41, Budapest V ☎ 266 4085

Living Room

A huge club with three rooms offering different music styles to dance to. The crowd is generally college age.

✉ Kossuth Lajos 17, Budapest V ☎ 06 70 337 3434

Negro

The city's most renowned cocktail bar is close to Szent István Bazilika (▶ 50) and has outdoor seating.

✉ Szent István tér 11, Budapest V ☎ 302 0136

Trocadero Café

Spacious café with pool tables and dancing on separate levels. Hot Latin salsa bands pocket the best of the clientele, and even dance classes are available.

✉ Szent István körút 13, Budapest V ☎ 06 30 987 7450

Fat Mo's

The weekend sees this elaborately furnished bar, with a prohibition-era theme, packed with visitors and executives. Its attractions are affordable Irish beers, decent bands and dancing.

✉ Nyári Pál utca 11, Budapest V ☎ 267 3199

LIVE ARTS

Aranytíz Cultural Centre

A stalwart supporter of Hungarian folk culture, the Aranytíz focuses its attention on traditional music and dance. Its Saturday Magyar táncház (Hungarian dance house) is a riotous event.

✉ Arany János utca 10, Budapest V ☎ 311 2248; www.aranytiz.hu

Jazz Garden

The unusual decor – a jungle of indoor plants and, bizarrely, twinkling stars embedded in the ceiling – takes nothing away from the quality jazz featured here.

✉ Veres Pálné utca 44A, Budapest V ☎ 266 7364

Katona József

Katona József has arguably the highest theatre credentials in the country. It performs both mainstream and alternative plays and its smaller venue, the Karma, stages equally fine performances.

✉ Petőfi Sándor utca 6, Budapest V ☎ 318 3725; www.szinhaz.hu/katona

Merlin International Theatre

Close to the centre of Pest, the Merlin is a magical little theatre that hosts a plethora of plays in English.

✉ Gerlóczy utca 4, Budapest V ☎ 318 9338; www.szinhaz.hu/merlin

Pesti Vigadó

The acoustics at this illustrious riverside venue have improved after recent renovations. Previous performers have included Liszt, Wagner, Bartók and von Karajan, and today dance recitals and cultural events can be seen alongside traditional classical music.

✉ Vigadó tér 2, Budapest V ☎ 318 9903

Szent István Bazilika

Evening performances (usually beginning at 7) of classical, choral and orchestral music in this richly decorated and ornate church (► 50–51).

✉ Szent István tér 1, Budapest I ☎ 311 0839

Térezváros, Erzsébetváros and Városliget

With splendid entertainment venues and dozens of restaurants, cafés and bars, the buzz of modern Budapest is loudest in Terézváros (Teresa Town) and Erzsébetváros (Elizabeth Town). Városliget (City Park), further to the east, is an outdoor oasis in a very urban stretch of Budapest. It is a place to relax, stroll, play and admire the few remaining tributes to the Magyar millennium celebrations of 1896.

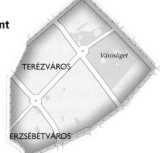

Terézváros and Erzsébetváros also have their fair share of history, dating mainly from periods in the 19th and 20th centuries when the area profited from boom times and suffered terribly under the Nazis. Terézváros is the more northerly of the two districts. Secessionist treasures hide in its back streets, while entertainment hot spots like the State Opera, Nagymező utca,

Budapest's Broadway, and Liszt Ferenc tér are situated closer to the Danube. Most of Erzsébetváros' attractions are close to central Pest, known locally as the old Jewish quarter. Here the last remnants of Budapest's Jewish community can be found along the likes of Dob and Kazincy utca.

Térezváros

ANDRÁSSY ÚT (ANDRÁSSY AVENUE)

Once the city's premier boulevard, it was named after the famous statesman Andrássy. An architectural jumble of glorious opulence and fading splendour, at one time it was known as Stalin Avenue, and until recently was called by the equally uninspiring name Avenue of the People's Republic. It runs all the way from City Park, and is home to the State Opera House and the Academy of Fine Arts, as well as to an almost constant stream of traffic, which makes walking a bit hectic. However, there are some good bargains here if you're in the mood to shop.

✚ 5H–9P ✉ Andrássy út, Budapest V 🍴 Baraka (€€€) 🚇 Oktogon

HOPP FERENC KELET-ÁZSIAI MÚZEUM
(FERENC HOPP MUSEUM OF EASTERN ASIATIC ART)

This museum, one of two in the city devoted to major collections of Asian art, houses the treasures amassed by the Hungarian traveller Ferenc Hopp (1833–1919), who once lived here. Like so many of the smaller and quirkier museums in the city, it's a little gem, and if nothing else tells you as much about Ferenc Hopp himself – a compulsive, eccentric collector – as about the treasures of East Asia. Among the fascinating ancient exhibits are Buddhist works and Indian art dating as far back as the 3rd century. A collection of Chinese and Japanese exhibits are housed nearby in the Ráth György Múzeum at 12 Városligeti fasor.

✚ 8Q ✉ Andrássy út 103, Budapest V ☎ 322 8476 🕐 Tue–Sun 10–6
🍴 Lukács (€) ✋ Inexpensive 🚇 M1 Bajza utca 🚌 Bus: red 4

LISZT FERENC EMLÉKMÚZEUM
(FERENC LISZT MEMORIAL MUSEUM)

In 1986, three rooms of the apartment where Liszt spent his last six years were turned into a museum celebrating his musical genius. Even though, by the looks of the static displays, little has changed since then, his musical library, original sheet music and black-and-white photos make good browsing for Liszt fans. The few highlights scattered throughout include Liszt's 'composing desk', sporting a three-octave keyboard, a piano with glass slices instead of strings and Liszt's warts-and-all death mask.

🚼 8R 🖂 Vörösmarty utca 35, Budapest VI ☎ 322 9804 🕓 Mon–Fri 10–6, Sat 9–5 🖐 Inexpensive 🍴 Lukács (€) 🚇 M1 Vörösmarty utca

MAGYAR ÁLLAMI OPERÁHAZ (STATE OPERA HOUSE)

Best places to see, ➤ 42–43.

NYUGATI PÁLYAUDVAR
(WESTERN RAILWAY STATION)

Since trains depart from here for the north and east, the name is perhaps slightly misleading. Constructed in the late 19th century, over the following 100 years the hall deteriorated and plans were drawn up for a new building. Conservationists protested and won the day, helping to preserve the principal iron structure. Towards the end of the hall on the left is a large door, above which is

carved the old Austro-Hungarian motto: *Viribus Units* (With Unity Strength). Beyond the door is the opulent Royal Lounge. The elegant glass screen of the station's main façade lets the trains merge with the city's traffic. The giant restaurant to the right of the main entrance is now a McDonald's, though they have retained the elegance of the room.

➕ 5F ✉ Teréz körút 55–57, Budapest VI ☎ Information: 349 0115 🕐 Open access ✋ Free 🍴 Nyugati (€) 🚇 Nyugati pályaudvar

POSTAMÚZEUM (POSTAL MUSEUM)

The Postal Museum was formerly a luxurious seven-room private apartment in the once affluent area of Sugarut. The owner's initials 'AS' (Andreás Saxlehner) can be seen all over the house. Most sumptuous of all are the impressive Károly Lotz frescoes on the staircase. Apart from the portable furniture most of the fittings and furniture are original. Attendants will put into operation some of the museum's exhibits. You can even see a section of a pneumatic exchange. An off-beat idea, but together with the other somewhat esoteric museums, it's what makes Budapest such a fascinating city.

➕ 5H ✉ Andrássy út 3, Budapest VI ☎ 269 6838 🕐 Tue–Sun 10–6 ✋ Inexpensive 🍴 Vista Café (€) 🚇 M1 Bajcsy-Zsilinszky út, M1/2/3 Deák tér 🚌 Bus: 105, red 4

TERROR HÁZA (HOUSE OF TERROR)

The hideous Russian tank crouched toadlike at the foot of the light well of this grim courtyard building on Andrássy út sets the tone for the horrifying tales recounted inside. Once the headquarters of the Arrow Cross, the home-grown Hungarian Nazis, after 1945 the edifice passed smoothly into the ownership of the Communist secret police.

Since 2002 it has housed sophisticated displays (with full commentaries in English) that expertly evoke some of the darker sides of Hungary's recent past: arbitrary rule, deportation,

genocide, forced resettlement, torture and murder.

A visit to the House of Terror is a sobering experience and an essential introduction to the country's tormented history in the 20th century, despite claims that the displays put excessive emphasis on Communist crimes and not enough on the atrocities of the Arrow Cross and Hungarian anti-Semitism.

🚼 7R ✉ Andrássy út 60 ☎ 374 2600 🕐 Tue–Fri 10–6, Sat, Sun 10–7:30 ✋ Expensive 🍴 Café (€–€€) 🚇 M1 Vörösmarty utca 🚌 Bus: 4

ZENEAKADÉMIA (ACADEMY OF MUSIC)

The Academy of Music, another of Miksa Róth's impressive art nouveau gems, was completed in 1907. Its first president was the great Hungarian composer Franz Liszt (a bronze statue of him stands above the main entrance), and its first director was Ferenc Erkel, the father of Hungarian grand opera. The main hall seats 1,200, and is dominated by the magnificent Walcker organ. On each side of the organ there are inscriptions in Latin: *Sursum Corda* (Raise Your Hearts) on the left; and *Favete Linguis* (Shut Up, or Be Quiet) on the right. A beautiful building, the Academy is the centre of Budapest's musical life.

🚼 7S ✉ Liszt Ferenc tér 8, Budapest VI ☎ 462 4600 🕐 From 10am to performance end ✋ Free 🍴 Menza (€€) 🚇 M1 Oktogon 🚋 Tram: 4, 6

Erzsébetváros

NAGY ZSINAGÓGA (GREAT SYNAGOGUE)

At the intersection of Dohány utca and Károly körút, at the heart of the old Jewish quarter, stands the Great Synagogue, the largest in Europe. Above the entrance the Hebrew line reads: 'Make me a sanctuary and I will dwell among them'. With its three naves and flat ceiling, the building holds 3,000 worshippers; 1,497 men on the ground floor and 1,472 women in the gallery.

One of the buildings in the compound was the birthplace of Theodor Herzl, the father of the Zionist movement. Built in Moorish-Byzantine style, the synagogue has two magnificent domes rising to 43m (141ft).

The Holocaust Memorial in the back garden is directly over the mass graves dug during the 1944–45 Hungarian Fascist period, and on every leaf is the name of a martyr. The memorial is a grim reminder of the suffering of the Hungarian Jews, and of their determination never to forget. The walls of some of the buildings near the synagogue still bear bullet marks.

➕ 6J ✉ Dohány utca 2–8, Budapest VII ☎ 342 8949

🕐 Mid-Apr to Oct Sun–Thu 10–5, Fri 10–2; Nov to mid-Apr Sun–Thu 10–3, Fri 10–2 💰 Expensive 🍴 Spinoza (€€–€€€) Ⓜ M2 Astòria 🚌 Bus: 7, 7/A, 78; tram: 47, 49; trolley bus: 74

NEW YORK KAVEHAZ (NEW YORK COFFEEHOUSE)

To some, the New York Coffeehouse is the pinnacle of Budapest's café culture, to others, it's an exaggerated eyesore; either way, there is no denying its history. Now part of a newly renovated five-star hotel, the New York began life in 1894 as part of the New York Palace. From its very beginning, it was *the* literary café, attracting the city's top writers and artists in droves. For decades it remained open day and night year-round until the threat of war and the 1930s depression forced its closure.

It remained closed until the 21st century and opened its doors after a complete refurbishment in Italian neo-Renaissance style. The café today lacks any warmth or cosiness – traits of a top coffeehouse – but it does have grandeur: a row of winged Pan statues adorns the façade, and the interior is embellished with plush red seating, frescoed ceilings, twisted gold columns, giant mirrors, and an army of chandeliers. The attached hotel is also worth a peek (➤ 151).

🚊 8T 🖂 Erzsébet körút 9–11, Budapest VII ☎ 886 6167; www.boscolohotels.com 🕙 Mon–Thu 10am–midnight, Fri–Sun 9am–midnight 🎟 Free 🚇 M2 Blaha Lujza tér

RÓTH MIKSA EMLÉKHÁZ (MIKSA ROTH MEMORIAL HOUSE)

Works by the prolific art nouveau artist Miksa Róth (1865–1944) can be seen at his former residence on Nefelejcs utca. Róth, who lived and worked here from 1911 till his death, is best known for his stunning stained-glass pieces, but he also created gorgeous mosaics which are displayed at the house.

The surprisingly bland living quarters are still filled with Roth's original furniture. Further examples of his genius are found around the city, at the Gresham Palace (➤ 122), the Országház (➤ 48), and the Zeneakadémia (➤ 141).

🚊 9S 🖂 Nefelejcs utca 26, Budapest VII ☎ 341 6789 🕙 Tue–Sat 2pm–6pm 🎟 Inexpensive 🚇 M2 Keleti pályaudvar

a walk around the VI District

The most illustrious part of the city in the late 19th century, the VI District is now a mixture of dilapidation and residual glamour.

Start at the State Opera House on Andrássy út.

Though often congested with traffic now, Andrássy út was once the Champs Elysées of Budapest, and its neo-Renaissance and baroque opera house (► 42) is one of the finest in Europe.

Walk up towards the Oktogon and look out for the magnificent Művész Coffee House and the Párizsi Nagyaruház at No 29.

The latter was once an exclusive casino, and some of its former glory remains.

Past the grand villas is the Lukács Coffee House, newly restored to its former splendour, and the Kodaly körönd, sumptuously painted with delicate gold filigree. After the Kodály körönd, go right along Bajza utca, past the old villas and diplomatic residences, to Városligeti fasor.

In the 19th century, this grand boulevard with tree-lined pavements (sidewalks) was used for horse-racing. Here at the boundary of the VI District you will see some wonderful art nouveau villas and mansions.

Take a quiet break in the Epreskert, or Mulberry Garden, half-way along Bajza utca.

This is the Arts Academy sculpture garden with both baroque sculptures and modern works.

Meander back via Király utca and Hunyadi tér to the heart of the district. At the intersection with Erszébet körút, turn right and head towards Liszt Ferenc tér on the left side.

Here is the Academy of Music (➤ 141), its magnificent concert hall a magnet for classical music lovers.

Turn left on to Andrássy út and return to the State Opera House.

Distance 4–5km (2.5–3 miles)
Time 2–3 hours, or 5 hours with stops for refreshments and visits
Start/end point State Opera House 🚩 5G 🚇 M1 Opera
Lunch Lukács (€) ✉ Andrássy út 70 ☎ 302 8747

Városliget

VÁROSLIGET (CITY PARK)

The City Park is the biggest of its kind in Budapest, where you can find just about every form of entertainment for children, as well as tranquillity for adults. Standing on an island in the boating lake is the fairy-tale Vajdahunyad Vár (Castle). Nearby, the beautiful art nouveau Állatkert (Zoo ➤ 62) is a perennial favourite with children, especially the 'Animal Kindergarten' where newborn animals are kept. Next to the Zoo is the Fővárosi Nagycirkusz (Municipal Circus, ► 62). The Vidámpark (Amusement Park, ► 63) is also very popular with a carousel, roller-coaster, Ferris wheel, an enchanted castle and a slot-machine hall.

The lavish **Széchenyi Gyógyfürdő** (thermal baths, ► 67) are the largest of their kind in Europe. Here you'll find the locals playing chess while relaxing in the thermal pools. There are various indoor and outdoor areas, but the outdoor baths with their whirlpools and shoulder-pounding fountains should not be missed.

Towards the southwest corner of the City Park is the Közlekedési Múzeum (Transport Museum, ► 149) and nearby the charming Garden for the Blind. Of interest also is Petőfi Csarnok (Hall) a bastion of rock and pop music. It also plays host to a flea market on weekends, a theatre for children, a roller-skating club, and a Saturday evening disco.

➕ Vajdahunyad Vár 10P; Állatkert 9P; Fővárosi Nagycirkusz 9N–10N; Vidámpark 10N; Közlekedési Múzeum11P; Petőfi Csarnok 10P

Széchenyi Gyógyfürdő

➕ 10N ✉ Állatkerti körút 11, Budapest XIV ☎ 363 3210 🕐 Daily 6am–10pm 💰 Expensive 🚇 M1 Széchenyi Fürdő

GUNDEL ÉTTEREM (GUNDEL RESTAURANT)

It's not unusual in Budapest to come across restaurants and cafés that are worth visiting not just for their food but also for their splendid architecture and décor. The unique thing about Gundel is its first-rate collection of Hungarian masters on the walls; the menu helpfully supplies information about the paintings. Above the splendid dining room are the Elisabeth and Andrássy rooms, where some of the most elegant banquets in Budapest are held. As you would expect, the food is excellent and there's a seriously well-stocked wine cellar to complement your meal.

➕ 9P ✉ Állatkerti kőrút 2, Budapest XIV ☎ 468 4040 🕐 Daily noon–2pm, 6:30am–midnight 🚇 M1 Hősök tér

HŐSÖK TERE (HEROES' SQUARE)

At the top of Andrássy út, where it meets City Park, is Heroes'
Square. The square forms a splendid unity of two architecturally
diverse buildings – the Art Gallery and the Museum of Fine Arts –
and a monument. The central feature of Heroes' Square is the
Millennium Monument, a 36m (118ft) column, on top of which
stands Gabriel, the Guardian Angel. The colonnades on either side

display statues of Hungarian kings and leading figures of the Hungarian independence wars. On the left wing are the allegorical bronze statues of War, Peace and Knowledge; on the right, statues representing War, Peace and Glory.

In the middle of the square, behind the column of Gabriel, is the picturesque group of statues of the conquering Magyars, with Árpád, the leading reigning prince, in the middle. The statue complex commemorates the 1,000th year of the Hungarian state. Dedicated to the nation's heroes, its architectural design is particularly fitting, and leaves you with a deep sense of Hungarians' pride in their past.

Next to Heroes' Square is Procession Square, where processions and parades are held on public holidays. This was the site of a monolithic statue of Stalin which was torn down by Hungarian nationalists during the 1956 Uprising. Also here is the Tomb of the Unknown Soldier, where Soviet veterans still come to pay their respects.

✚ 9P ✉ Budapest XIV 🕓 Open access 🍴 Robinson (€€–€€€) 🎫 Free
🚇 M1 Hősök tere 🚌 Bus: 20, 30; red 4; trolley: 75, 79

KÖZLEKEDÉSI MÚZEUM (TRANSPORT MUSEUM)

The exhibits include beautifully accurate models as well as examples of the real thing: ships, cars, motorbikes, and locomotives and rolling stock. A spacious hall 200m (219yds) from the main building houses several dozen aeroplanes and fascinating aviation memorabilia. The museum has a number of outstations including a display of commercial aircraft at Ferihegy airport (➤ 26).

✚ 11P ✉ Városligeti körút 11, Budapest XIV ☎ 273 3840 🕓 May–Sep Tue–Fri 10–5, Sat, Sun 10–6; Oct–Apr Tue–Fri 10–4, Sat, Sun 10–5 🎫 Free
🍴 Railway car (€) 🚌 Tram: 1; trolley bus: 70, 72, 74

SZÉPMŰVÉSZETI MÚZEUM (FINE ARTS MUSEUM)

Best places to see, ➤ 52–53.

HOTELS

Andrássy Hotel (€€€)

Just off the prestigous Andrássy út, this tasteful, luxurious hotel was once the exclusive guest house of the Foreign Ministry.

✉ Andrássy út 111, Budapest VI ☎ 462 2100; www.andrassyhotel.com

Corinthia Grand Hotel Royal (€€€)

Originally built at the time of the millennium celebrations in 1896, this city institution on the Outer Ring was reopened in 2003 in all its former glory. A tasteful combination of tradition and modernity.

✉ Erzsébet körút 43–49, Budapest VII ☎ 479 4000; www.corinthiahotels.com

Hotel Pest (€€)

An 18th-century townhouse in suburban Pest with simple, modern rooms. Within strolling distance to the Magyar Állami Operaház (➤ 42), bar-clad Liszt Ferenc tér, and the highlights of Belváros.

✉ Paulay Ede utca 31, Budapest VI ☎ 343 1198; www.hotelpest.hu

K + K Hotel Opera (€€)

This hotel was specially built for music lovers and is situated just 50m (55yds) from the Opera House. Guests are treated to immaculate service and can make use of the leisure facilities.

✉ Révay útca 24, Budapest VI ☎ 269 0222; www.kkhotels.com

Liget Hotel (€€)

The Liget is a reasonably priced three-star hotel in a prime position overlooking both the Fine Arts Museum (➤ 52) and zoo (➤ 62).

✉ Dózsa György út 106, Budapest VI ☎ 269 5300; www.liget.hu

Mamaison Residence Izabella (€€€)

Spacious apartments with wooden floors and modern amenities. Many face the quiet courtyard and offer private balconies.

✉ Izabella utca 61, Budapest VI ☎ 475 5900; www.residenceizabella.com

Medosz (€)

Basic accommodation, still breathing the atmosphere of the not-so-good old days pre-1989 when it provided lodgings for provincial trade unionists and the party faithful summoned to the metropolis. Great location near the Opera and nightlife on Liszt Ferenc tér.

✉ Jókai tér 9, Budapest VI ☎ 374 3001; www.medoszhotel.hu

Mercure Metropol (€)

This 100-room hotel in a busy downtown setting has basic facilities but is reasonably comfortable.

✉ Rákóczi út 58, Budapest VII ☎ 462 8100;www.mercure-metropole.hu

New York Palace (€€€)

This luxury establishment sports immaculate rooms filled with delicate antiques, fine art, and the latest hotel technology. Attached is the New York Kávéház (➤ 143).

✉ Erzsébet körút 9–11, Budapest VII ☎ 886 6167; www.boscolohotels.com

Radio Inn (€)

Spacious apartments in the quiet leafy diplomatic district near the city centre, with good public transport.

✉ Benczur utca 19, Budapest VI ☎ 342 8347; www.radioinn.hu

Radisson SAS Béke (€€)

A large modernized hotel on the city's main thoroughfare, the Grand Boulevard. Good eating can be had in the Szondi Lugas restaurant, with a pleasant café serving sweets and espresso.

✉ Teréz körút 43, Budapest VI ☎ 889 3900; www.radissonsas.com

Spinoza Apartments (€)

Known more for its cuisine and live music (➤ 154), Spinoza has branched out into the accommodation business with simple, clean, and comfy apartments at very affordable prices.

✉ Dob utca 15, Budapest VII ☎ 491 7069; www.spinozahaz.hu

RESTAURANTS

1894 Food & Wine Cellar (€€)

This bricked cellar restaurant focuses most of its attention on wine, but also serves fine traditional Hungarian and a smattering of international dishes. Set menus and wine tastings are offered.

✉ Állakertí út 2, Budapest XII ☎ 468 4040 🍴 Dinner. Closed Sun

Abszint (€€)

This simple yet stylish restaurant has an international menu blessed with a strong southern-French influence, and the head chef includes seasonal dishes on a regular basis.

✉ Andrássy út 34, Budapest VI ☎ 332 4993 ⏲ Lunch, dinner

Arigato (€€)

Arigato is a small family-run Japanese restaurant with an extensive selection of sushi, tempura, and udon and soba noodle soups.

✉ Ó utca 3, Budapest VI ☎ 353 3549 ⏲ Lunch, dinner. Closed Sun

Bagolyvár (€€)

Attached Gundel restaurant, the 'Owl Castle' provides 'homestyle' Hungarian food served in a convivial atmosphere.

✉ Állatkerti út 2, Budapest VI ☎ 468 3110 ⏲ Lunch, dinner

Baraka (€€€)

The resident restaurant of Andrássy Hotel, Baraka has a wildly inviting menu including dishes such as red snapper, wild duck breast, and crusted baked salmon in green curry.

✉ Andrássy út 111, Budapest VI ☎ 483 1355 ⏲ Lunch, dinner

Belcanto (€€)

This restaurant is by the State Opera House and its waiters sing from well-known operas. Good international cuisine.

✉ Dalszinház utca 8, Budapest VI ☎ 269 2786 ⏲ Lunch, dinner

Bouchon (€€–€€€)

Bouchon's modern Hungarian menu easily stirs the appetite; you'll find roasted goose liver, steamed pike-perch with vegetables and rosemary-saffron potatoes, and roasted veal 'Shaslik' with garlic and spicy mixed salad. Local wine also features heavily.

✉ Zichy Jenő utca 33, Budapest VI ☎ 353 4094 ⏲ Lunch, dinner. Closed Sun

Chez Daniel (€€)

A small, select menu of excellent French dishes is carefully and affectionately prepared. Good wine and beer list. Book ahead.

✉ Sziv utca 32, Budapest VI ☎ 302 4039 🕐 Lunch, dinner

Fausto's (€€€)

Ranks among the best restaurants in the city, and serves creative Italian dishes in stylish surroundings. It's best to rely on the knowledgeable staff to choose your wine from the huge list here.

✉ Dohány utca 5, Budapest VII ☎ 269 6808 🕐 Lunch, dinner. Closed Sun

Gundel (€€€)

Hungary's most famous restaurant, situated on the edge of City Park by the Zoological Gardens. The Gundel has been restored to its *fin de siècle* splendour, and smart dress is required.

✉ Állatkerti út 3, Budapest XIV ☎ 468 4040 🕐 Lunch, dinner. Brunch Sun

Hanna (€€)

Immerse yourself further in the ambience of the Jewish Quarter by having a tasty kosher lunch in the light and airy dining hall attached to the Orthodox synagogue. Cash only.

✉ Dob utca 35, Budapest VII ☎ 342 1072 🕐 Lunch only

Kispapa (€€€)

Stiff but attentive service, old fashioned Hungarian and international cuisine, and live piano music (from 7pm).

✉ Akácfa utca 38, Budapest VII ☎ 342 2587 🕐 Lunch, dinner

Marquis de Salade (€€)

A unique animal in Budapest, Marquis de Salade specializes in Azerbaijani food. There are Russian and Hungarian dishes thrown into the mix, and vegetarians will be ecstatic with the menu too.

✉ Hajós utca 43, Budapest VI ☎ 302 4086 🕐 Lunch, dinner

Menza (€€)

The retro regime of 60s floral wallpaper, plastic booths and Formica finish is a refreshing change from Liszt Ferenc tér's swathe of modern establishments. Young socialites and business-lunchers flock here for Hungarian standards with a modern twist.

✉ Liszt Ferenc tér 2, Budapest VI ☎ 413 1482 🕐 Lunch, dinner

Napos Oldal (€)

This health-food café is named after the side of the street on which it sits. Staff are super-friendly, and the fresh vegetarian salads and pastries are a welcome change from Hungarian fare.

✉ Jókai utca 7, Budapest VI ☎ 312 3145 ⏰ Lunch Mon–Sat, dinner Mon–Fri

Premier (€€€)

This time-honoured restaurant of Budapest's dining scene has Hungarian dishes and a smattering of international choices. Its art nouveau cellar comes complete with stained-glass windows.

✉ Andrássy út 101, Budapest VI ☎ 342 1768 ⏰ Lunch, dinner

Robinson (€€)

The Robinson is romantically located on the lake by Heroes' Square, a feature reflected in the prices. The menu is not extensive, but don't miss 'Robinson Palacsinta,' a crêpe filled with vanilla cream and fresh-fruit salad. Business lunches.

✉ Városliget Lake, Budapest XIV ☎ 422 0222 ⏰ Lunch, dinner

Sir Lancelot (€)

Enormous portions are served on wooden plates by waiters in period costume. Live Renaissance music in the evenings.

✉ Podmaniczky utca 14, Budapest VI ☎ 302 4456 ⏰ Lunch, dinner

Spinoza (€€–€€€)

This polished eatery in the heart of the Jewish District serves Hungarian and Jewish dishes in relaxed surroundings. There's also theatre and live music some nights.

✉ Dob utca 15, Budapest VII ☎ 413 7488 ⏰ Lunch, dinner

CAFÉS

Café Vian

Vian has a lively buzz and excellent desserts. Floor to ceiling windows in winter and pavement seating in summer allow unabridged views of Liszt Ferenc tér. Pick up a coffee or cocktail and watch the comings and goings.

✉ Liszt Ferenc tér 9, Budapest VI ☎ 268 1154

Lukács

Almost everything about Lukács is refined, from its evening pianist to its divine selection of cakes and elegant turn-of-the-century interior.

✉ Andrássy út 70, Budapest VI ☎ 302 8747

Mai Manó

This tiny café has a North-African look and a healthy local following. It's a fine place to linger over coffee or wine while enjoying the sights on theatrical Nagymező utca.

✉ Nagymező utca 20, Budapest VI ☎ 473 2666

Művész

Művész ('artist') is a century-old café with classical trimmings – delectable desserts, fin-de-siècle decor, and waiters with expressions that could curdle your coffee's milk at twenty paces.

✉ Andrássy út 29, Budapest VI ☎ 352 1337

New York

This splendid and famous old establishment was restored to its former state and reopened in 2004 as part of a new luxury hotel.

✉ Erzsébet Körút 9–11, Budapest VII ☎ 429 5500

Vista Café

A café and restaurant with internet access and tourist information. Contemporary, tasty international cuisine and jazz most weekends.

✉ Paulay Ede utca 7, Budapest VII ☎ 268 0888

SHOPPING

Classic Line

Famous designer clothes for women and men. An elegant and exclusive shop offering the latest international fashions.

✉ Andrássy út 28, Budapest VI ☎ 331 2837

Concerto Records

An extensive range of second-hand and new classical music.

✉ Dob utca 33, Budapest VII ☎ 268 9631

Helikon

A lavishly decorated bookshop with a comprehensive selection of Hungarian and foreign books. Small café in the basement.

✉ Bajcsy-Zsilinszky út 37, corner Hajós utca, Budapest VI ☎ 331 2329

Judaica Gallery

One of the very few shops selling items related to the Jewish culture in Hungary.

✉ Wesselényi utca 13, Budapest VII ☎ 267 8502

Tisza Cipő

The communist-era sportswear sold here is all the go in Budapest.

✉ Károly körút 1, Budapest VII ☎ 266 3055

Wave

An excellent selection of home-grown music.

✉ Révay köz 2, Budapest VI ☎ 331 6431

ENTERTAINMENT

NIGHTLIFE

Angyal

'Angel' is Budapest's most established gay bar, with men only on Saturday but mixed the rest of the week.

✉ Kazinczy utca 2, Budapest VII ☎ 351 6490

Bahnhof

Bahnhof is big and has a railroad theme. Two dance floors for rock and disco (no techno), and live acts. Cover charge.

✉ Váci út 1, Budapest VI ☎ 302 4571

Bamboo Club

Tropical-theme bar playing retro disco, funk and soul. Cover charge.

✉ Dessewffy utca 44, Budapest VI ☎ 428 2225

Benczúr Club

A good club for serious music fans. Live music Wednesday to Sunday after 7pm. Wednesday it's jazz; Thursday to Saturday live blues, rock and alternative; Sunday classical. Cover charge.

✉ Benczúr utca 27, Budapest VI ☎ 321 7334

Fészek Club

An occasionally crazy club with a lively vibe and plenty of late-night drinkers. The cellar bar has cushioned booths and a small stage.

✉ Kertész utca 36, Budapest VII ☎ 342 6549 ⏰ 8pm–5am

Karma

A confused pseudo-Asian bar that gets rave reviews from locals. Low couches and cushioned corners occupy the rear of the establishment, while tables and high bar stools take up the front.

✉ Liszt Ferenc tér 11, Budapest VI ☎ 413 6764

Old Man's Music Pub

Designed like a faded living room, the Old Man's Pub features blues and folk nightly, with good pizzas and other dishes on the menu.

✉ Akácfa utca13, Budapest VII ☎ 322 7645

Piaf

Named after the French singer, this basic club attracts a slightly more mature crowd.

✉ Nagymező utca 25, Budapest VI ☎ 312 3823

Pótkulcs

Hidden behind a nondescript fence, the 'Spare Key' is a welcoming bar filled with sagging furniture and a relaxed crowd.

✉ Csengery 65/b, Budapest VI ☎ 269 1050

Sark

A fine bohemian haunt to while away a few hours. Staff often insist you at least learn a little Hungarian for ordering drinks.

✉ Klauzál tér 14, Budapest ☎ 328 0753

Sixtus

Friendly staff, boisterous regulars and an eclectic range of music.

✉ Nagy Diófa utca 26–28 ☎ 413 6722

Szimpla
This lovely bohemian bar with worn wooden floors and a rabble of mis-matching furniture covers three levels.
✉ Kertész utca 48, Budapest VII ☎ 321 9119

LIVE ARTS
Magyar Állami Operház (State Opera House)
World opera at one of the finest and most beautiful opera houses in Europe. Suitable for the aficionado and amateur alike (➤ 42).
✉ Andrássy út 22, Budapest VI ☎ 3533 0170

Radnóti
An established theatre that hosts classical and contemporary works plus lighter musical comedies. Open October to May.
✉ Nagymező utca 11, Budapest VI ☎ 321 0600; www.radnotiszinhaz.hu

Opperettszínház (Operetta Theatre)
The unrivalled venue for the best of Hungarian operetta and not to be missed.
✉ Pest VI Nagymező utca 19 ☎ 312 4866

Central Europe Dance Theatre
Folk and contemporary dance performances representing regional culture are staged here.
✉ Bethlen Gábor tér 3, Budapest VII ☎ 342 7163

Petőfi Csarnok
Petőfi Csarnok hosts medium-sized rock concerts in Városliget.
✉ Zichy Mihály út 14, Budapest XIV ☎ 363 3730; www.petoficsarnok.hu

Zeneakadémia (Academy of Music)
Glorious art nouveau architecture, fine acoustics and frequent classical concerts in a superlative venue.
✉ Liszt Ferenc tér 8, Budapest VI ☎ 342 0179

CHILDREN'S ENTERTAINMENT
See page 62.

Józsefváros and Ferencváros

Józsefváros (Joseph Town) and Ferencváros (Francis Town) have the same general make-up – solidly working class with a large dose of grit. Many buildings, particularly west of Pest's big ring road Nagykörút, are in a run-down state, but among the dilapidated dwellings are a handful of superb museums and state-of-the-art concert and theatre halls.

To the north, Józsefváros is largely bereft of sights aside from the excellent Magyar Nemzeti Múzeum (Hungarian National Museum ➤ 160) and peaceful Kerepesi temető (Kerepes Cemetery ➤ 160).

Ferencváros is almost double the size of Józsefváros but much

of its southern extreme is of little interest, criss-crossed by rail tracks and dotted with industrial sites. Inside the Nagykörút is another matter; this urban playground is home to the Vásárcsarnok (Central Market Hall ➤ 165), the Iparművészeti Múzeum (Museum of Applied Arts ➤ 162), and restaurant-studded Ráday utca. Two of the city's newest cultural venues, the Művészetek Palotája (Palace of Arts ➤ 164) and Nemzeti Színház (National Theatre ➤ 165) are also here.

Józsefváros

KEREPESI TEMETŐ (KEREPES CEMETERY)

Kerepes is the official burial place of the Hungary's national heroes. The largest mausoleums belong to Lajos Batthyány, Ferenc Deák and Lajos Kossuth. Batthyány, the first prime minister of Hungary, is honoured by a wide set of stairs guarded by lions, while Kossuth, a seminal leader in the 1848–49 War of Independence, is entombed in an enormous stone pagoda structure. The most central of the three, to Deák, an important statesman during the Dual Monarchy, is a domed affair topped by a wreath-bearing angel. Other noteworthy figures buried in the cemetery include the poets Endre Ady and Attila József, architects Ödön Lechner and Alajos Stróbl, and actress Lujza Blaha. Near the gate is the massive Pantheon to the Working Class Movement, used as a burial ground for the country's socialist leaders; the inscription above the mausoleum reads 'They lived for communism and the people'.

✚ 11U ✉ Fiumei út 16, Budapest VIII ☎ 333 9125 ⊗ May–Jul daily 7am–8pm; Apr, Aug 7–7; Sep 7–6; Mar, Oct 7–5; Nov–Feb 7.30–5 ⦿ Free ⦿ Astoria, Kálvin tér ⦿ Tram: 24, 28

MAGYAR NEMZETI MÚZEUM (HUNGARIAN NATIONAL MUSEUM)

The dignified neoclassical building set back in its own gardens is a dominant feature on the city's inner ring boulevard, Múzeum körút. It was completed in 1847, just in time for the ardent rebels of 1848 to use its broad steps as a platform for proclaiming their revolution with a spirited rendering of the *National Song*, composed for the occasion by the young poet Sándor Petőfi.

Inside are a central rotunda, a dome and a magnificent double staircase with wall-paintings.

A treasure-house of every kind of artefact, the museum gives a comprehensive and fascinating account of the course of Hungarian history and prehistory.

A section entitled 'On the East–West Frontier' traces the evolution of the inhabitants of the Carpathian Basin from 400,000BC to AD804. A variety of up-to-the-minute techniques enlivens the story. You can see the reconstruction of a 6,000-year-old house, walk over prehistoric skeletons in their graves and confront a Bronze Age warrior with sword and helmet.

The rich and extensive displays illustrating Hungarian history since the conversion to Christianity of King Stephen in 1000 are more static, but no less intriguing.

➕ 6K ✉ Múzeum körút 14–16, Budapest VIII ☎ 338 2122; www.hnm.hu
🕐 Tue–Sun 10–6 💷 Free 🚇 M2 Astoria, M3 Kálvin tér
🚌 Bus: 9; tram: 47, 49

MAGYAR TERMÉSZETTUDOMÁNYI MÚZEUM (HUNGARIAN NATURAL HISTORY MUSEUM)

A fun excursion for those with kids in tow. A huge whale gliding above the foyer is a sign of things to come. To the right once you enter the museum proper is an underwater hall with fresh- and saltwater aquariums and a coral-reef display under glass flooring.

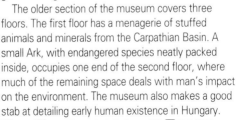

The older section of the museum covers three floors. The first floor has a menagerie of stuffed animals and minerals from the Carpathian Basin. A small Ark, with endangered species neatly packed inside, occupies one end of the second floor, where much of the remaining space deals with man's impact on the environment. The museum also makes a good stab at detailing early human existence in Hungary.

➕ 10W ✉ Ludovika tér 2–6, Budapest VIII ☎ 210 1085
🕐 Wed–Mon 10–6 🍴 Café (€) 💷 Permanent exhibitions: free; temporary exhibitions: expensive 🚇 M3 Klinikák

Ferencváros

HOLOKAUSZT MÚZEUM (HOLOCAUST MUSEUM)

Opened in 2004 on the site of a synagogue all but destroyed in
World War II, the centre is an exhibition space and education
facility funded by the government. The modern structure is split
into three parts: a reconstructed synagogue where temporary
exhibitions are held; a new wing containing the permanent 'From
Deprivation of Rights to Genocide'; and a Memorial Wall engraved
with the names of holocaust victims.

The permanent exhibition spotlights the plight of Jews, Roma
and other persecuted persons during the Nazi regime, but
primarily focuses on three families. Photos, videos and private
effects line the walls, providing a very personal account of the
holocaust. Each room deals with the ever-increasing phases of
persecution; from the deprivation of rights, to property, freedom,
human dignity, and finally life. Audio guides (500Ft) are useful but
not essential as English descriptions are found throughout.

🚩 8W ⊠ Páva utca 39, Budapest IX ☎ 455 3333 🕐 Tue–Sun 10–6
🅿 Moderate 🍴 Claro Bisztró (€) 🚇 M3 Ferenc körút

IPARMŰVÉSZETI MÚZEUM
(MUSEUM OF APPLIED ARTS)

This fine museum was rebuilt in the 1950s after it was destroyed,
during World War II. The original building was in fact one of
hundreds hastily built to mark the millennial celebrations of 1896.
The coloured ceramic-and-brick building blends an art nouveau
style with Hungarian folk motifs, which makes it a museum piece
in itself. The main hall is covered with a steel-framed glass ceiling.

If you can pull yourself away from its décor, there are fine
collections of furniture, metalwork, textiles, woodwork, ceramics
and glass to be seen, as well as examples of other handicrafts.

🚩 8W ⊠ Üllői út 33–7, Budapest IX ☎ 456 5100; www.imm.hu 🍴 Soul
Café (€€) 🕐 Tue–Sun 10–6 🅿 Expensive 🚇 M3 Ferenc körút 🚊 Tram: 4, 6

MUVÉSZETEK PALOTÁJA (PALACE OF ARTS) AND
LUDWIG MÚZEUM BUDAPEST

Opened in March 2005, the Palace of Arts, which incorporates the Ludwig Museum Budapest, is the city's latest cultural offering. For some it's also the greatest, for it is home to the National Philharmonic, National Dance Theatre and contemporary art in Budapest; it also shares a lonely stretch of the Pest embankment with the Nemzeti Színház. Architecturally, it is quite bland, but its performance halls are exceptional, employing the latest technology to create the finest acoustics in the city.

The Ludwig covers three floors in the Palace's western wing with the city's premiere collection of contemporary art. Hungarian

artists feature strongly, but it's the big international names that steal the show; look for Andy Warhol's *Single Elvis* (1964), Pablo Picasso's *Musketeer with Sword* (1972), Roy Lichtenstein's *Vicki* (1964) and Chuck Close's *Nat* (1972–73. The museum's calendar features temporary exhibitions of both current artists from Hungary and abroad, although it mainly focuses on the exposure of Central and Eastern European artists.

✚ 8Z ✉ Komor Marcell utca 1, Budapest IX ⏹ Café (€)

🚌 Tram: 2, 24

Muvészetek Palotája

☎ 555 3000; www.mupa.hu ⏱ Ticket office Mon–Fri 1–6, Sat, Sun 10–6

Ludwig Múzeum Budapest

☎ 555 3444; www.lumu.org.hu ⏱ Tue–Sun 10–8

✋ Permanent exhibitions: free; temporary exhibitions: expensive

NEMZETI SZÍNHÁZ (NATIONAL THEATRE)

Opened in 2002 as the focal point of a new 'Millennium City Centre' in an inconvenient out-of-town site by the Danube, the lavish new National Theatre is worth a look for its sheer size, its weird mixture of styles, its brash statuary and its odd landscaping.

✚ 8Z ✉ Bajor Gizi Park, Budapest IX ☎ 476 6800 🚌 Tram: 2

VÁSÁRCSARNOK (CENTRAL MARKET HALL)

The Central Market Hall is all you could ever wish of a market place – full of the aromas of fresh vegetables, fish, hung sausages, cheeses and flowers, with beautiful folk art handicrafts. And on the lower floor is the Pick Market, a mingling of modern supermarket and the bargain-basement stall. The best bargain is a beer and snack at one of the small bars on the upper floor.

✚ 5L ✉ Vámház körút 1–3, Budapest IX ☎ 366 3300

⏱ Mon 6am–5pm, Tue–Fri 6–6, Sat 6–2. Closed Sun ✋ Free

⏹ Market hall food bars (€) 🚌 Tram: 2, 47, 49; trolley bus: 83

HOTELS

Hotel Sissi (€€)

Aside from the antique-clad Sissi Room, the hotel's namesake – the much-beloved 19th-century Habsburg Empress Sissi – barely surfaces in this modern hotel. Rooms are spartan, clean and occasionally come with balcony, and the neighbourhood is quiet.

✉ Angyal utca 33, Budapest IX ☎ 215 0082; www.hotelsissi.hu

Ibis Centrum (€€)

Just off the city centre and close to the shopping and business areas, the hotel has 126 rooms which benefit from soundproofed windows. It has a garage and a roof garden.

✉ Ráday utca 6, Budapest IX ☎ 456 4100; www.ibis-centrum.hu

Mercure Nemzeti (€€)

Traditional splendour of the Grand Boulevard days is available here with 76 rooms, suites and a conference room. However, the hotel is built over an underground station, Blaha Lujza tér.

✉ József körút 4, Budapest VIII ☎ 477 2000; www.mercure-nemzeti.hu

RESTAURANTS

Costes (€€–€€€)

A stylish restaurant/bar with an inviting menu of carefully prepared modern Hungarian and international cuisine.

✉ Ráday utca 4, Budapest XI ☎ 219 0696 🕐 Lunch, dinner

Fülemüle (€€)

This lovely Jewish (but not kosher) restaurant specializes in goose, but also offers meat, fish and other poultry; vegetarians however will have to settle for grilled cheese and salads.

✉ Kőfaragó utca 5, Budapest VIII ☎ 266 7947 🕐 Lunch, dinner

Múzeum (€€)

Múzeum is still going strong after over a hundred years in business and serves solid Hungarian fare in beautifully preserved *fin-de-siècle* surroundings.

✉ Múzeum körút 12, Budapest VIII ☎ 267 0375 🕐 Lunch, dinner

Pata Negra (€€)

The 'Black Hoof' is the only authentic tapas bar in Budapest. Order a bottle of Rioja and begin sampling from the selection of around 40 tapas, or simply snack away on cheese and olives.

✉ Kálvin tér 8, Budapest IX ☎ 215 5616 🕐 Lunch, dinner

Pink Cadillac (€€)

Pink Cadillac isn't sophisticated, but it is a fun date. The menu selection – whether it be pizzas, pastas or salads – is extensive and the service quick and friendly.

✉ Ráday utca 22, Budapest IX ☎ 216 1412 🕐 Lunch, dinner

Soul Café (€)

On a street bustling with recently opened restaurants and bars. It has a good atmosphere and tasty Mediterranean cuisine.

✉ Ráday utca 11–13, Budapest IX ☎ 217 6986 🕐 Lunch, dinner

CAFÉS

Café Csiga

Small Csiga is a proper locals' café with a cosy ambience and eclectic décor. Choose from a stool at the bar or a table by the window and watch the activity on nearby Rákóczi tér.

✉ Vásár utca 2, Budapest VIII ☎ 210 0885

Hauer Cukrászda

Hauer has seen better days since it opened in 1890, but it still retains a semblance of grace. It bakes a lengthy list of cakes and pastries, including Sacher torte, truffle tart and Russian cream tart.

✉ Rákóczi út 47–49 Budapest VIII ☎ 323 1476

SHOPPING

FOOD AND DRINK

Ági Gyümölcs Greengrocers

A small corner shop that reputedly offers the freshest and best-quality produce in the area. Family photographs adorn the wall, interspersed with some motorcycle advertisements.

✉ Tátra utca 20, Budapest XIII

Magyar Pálinka Ház
Sells varieties of *pálinka*, Hungary's version of fruit brandy.
✉ Rákóczi út 17, Budapest VIII ☎ 338 4219 🕐 Sat–Sun 6–5

Vásárcsarnok
See page 165.

ENTERTAINMENT

NIGHTLIFE

Claro Bisztró
Claro has a convivial vibe and attracts an easy-going clientele.
Walls are decorated with posters of film classics, the layout is
open and airy, and most nights it's free of smoke.
✉ Ráday utca 35, Budapest IX ☎ 216 1577

Darshan Udvar
This collection of two bars, a café and a restaurant all huddled
around a North African-themed inner courtyard is the heart of
Krúdy utca's nightlife.
✉ Krúdy utca 7, Budapest VIII ☎ 266 5541

E–Klub
Despite a jaded ambience, good live acts perform in the main hall
with mixed music and DJs on the dance floors.
✉ Népliget, Budapest X ☎ 263 1614

Kultiplex
Kultiplex is not only a centre for alternative and fringe acts, but
also for film, top DJs, football broadcasts, and organized parties.
✉ Kinizsi utca 28, Budapest IX ☎ 219 0706

Trafó Bár Tangó
Filling the basement of the Trafó Kortárs Művészetek Háza (below),
this long bar attracts an arty-party crowd with its sleek look and
locally renowned DJs, with jazz to alternative on the turntables.
✉ Liliom utca 41, Budapest IX ☎ 456 2049; www.trafo.hu

West Balkan

West Balkan is an excellent, easy-going club with quality DJs and a tree-shaded courtyard in summer.

✉ Kisfaludy utca 36, Budapest VIII ☎ 371 1807

LIVE ARTS
Mıvészetek Palotája
See page 164.

Nemzeti Színház
See page 165.

Trafó Kortárs Mıvészetek Háza (Trafó House of Contemporary Arts)

This former electrical transformer station hosts contemporary performances including dance, theatre, music and readings.

✉ Liliom utca 41, Budapest IX ☎ 456 2040; www.trafo.hu

CHILDREN'S ENTERTAINMENT
Hungarian Natural History Museum
See page 165.

Csodák Palotája: Interaktív Tudományos Játszóház (Palace of Wonders: Interactive Scientific Playhouse)
See page 62.

Planetárium
See page 63.

SPORT
Billiards

You can play billiards in almost 100 venues around the city, mainly in pubs and clubs. The few dedicated billiard halls include:

Atlantis

✉ Váci út 156, Budapest XIII ☎ 349 4946

Black Pool

✉ Vámház körút 15, Budapest IX ☎ 218 9379

Excursions

There's plenty to do beyond central Budapest. Easily reached by public transport is the Statue Park and Buda Hills, the first a display station for unwanted communist memorials, the second a string of wooded hills popular with walkers and cyclists. With a little more effort the pretty towns along the Danube to the north of Budapest can be explored. This stretch of the river is known as the Danube Bend, where rising hills have forced the river into sharp turns. Here you'll find Esztergom, home of the Roman Catholic church for 1,000 years, Visegrád, location of the ruins of King Mátyás' medieval Royal Palace, and Szentendre, famous for its religious freedom and former artists' colony. Not far east of the capital is Gödöllő, home to an exceptional baroque palace built in the mid-18th century. Note that traffic out of the city can be particularly heavy on Fridays, when many Pestians migrate to the countryside.

City outskirts

BUDAI-HEGYEK (BUDA HILLS)

The Buda Hills are Budapest's largest outdoor playground and stretch to well within the city's borders. They're not massive – the tallest peaks are just over 500m (1,640ft) – but they offer a quick escape from urban living and a chance to breathe clean, fresh air. And with a few quirky transport choices, getting there is half the fun. Two tram stops from Buda's Moszkva tér is the Fogaskerekű vasút (Cog Railway), a fun but occasionally jarring way up into the hills. When completed in 1874, it ran on steam. For the best views, sit on the right-hand side facing backwards. The railway is included in the city's transport tickets.

Only a short walk from the Cog Railway's final stop is another unusual railway, the Gyermekvasút (Children's Railway). This narrow-gauge rail was built in 1948 by the socialist version of the Scouts and is still run almost solely by enthusiastic children between the ages of 10 and 14. The dinky little train winds its way through wooded hills to Hűvösvölgy about 12km (7.5 miles) from its starting point (40-minute journey). Disembark at János-hegy for Erzsébet-kilátó (Elizabeth Tower), the hill's highest point at 527m (1,876ft), and yet another unusual transport option, the **Libegő** (Chair lift).

One of the few museums in the hills is the **Bartók Béla Emlékház** (Béla Bartók Memorial House), devoted to one of Hungary's greatest musicians.

🚊 Tram: 18, 56 from II Moszkva tér (on the M2 line) lead directly into the Buda Hills and call at the Cog Railway en-route

Libegő

✉ Jánoshegyi/Zugligeti út

🕐 Mid-May to mid-Sep daily 9:30–5; mid-Sep to mid-May daily 9:30–4:30

✋ Inexpensive

Bartók Béla Emlékház

✉ Csalán út 29 ☎ 394 2100; www.bartokmuseum.hu

🕐 Tue–Sun 10–5 ✋ Moderate

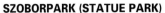

SZOBORPARK (STATUE PARK)

Statue Park is home to more than 40 statues which graced the cityscape during the communist era. Since its opening in 1993, it has been a popular – and surreal – attraction on the outskirts of Budapest.

Enormous statues of Lenin, Marx and Engels greet visitors to the park. Inside, the remaining 39 statues are laid out in semi-circles, and almost all are a uniform dark grey, with patches of pale green where the metal's outer shell has worn thin. Easily the most impressive statue is Imre Varga's Béla Kun memorial (statue No 24); this bronze, copper and steel piece shows Kun directing soldiers into the fray. Other striking examples include the massive – and powerful – Republics of Councils monument (statue No 33) and the memorial to the Hungarian freedom-fighters who fought in the Spanish civil war (statue No 32).

Despite their intended purpose, other statues appear almost comical; a cricket fielder stretches for a spectacular catch (Martyrs monument, statue No 38) and a lollipop man prepares to stop traffic at a pedestrian crossing (Osztapenkó, statue No 41). The park's shop sells bizarre Soviet souvenirs such as Lenin and Stalin candles, communist pocket watches, and Best of Communism CDs.

www.szoborpark.hu

✉ Corner Balatoni út and Szabadkai utca, Budapest XXII

☎ 227 7446 🕐 Daily 10am–sunset 💷 Moderate

🚌 Bus: Direct services run from the corner of V. Deák Ferenc tér and Harmincad utca. Cheaper buses leave from Etele tér, Budapest XI: catch a yellow Volán bus from stand 7 to Diósd-Érd and ask the driver to let you off at the park

Further afield

ESZTERGOM

Birthplace of King Stephen I, this is one of Hungary's most historically important and fascinating cities. Its history dates back to Roman times when one of its most renowned visitors, Marcus Aurelius, camped here. Sadly, much of the original city was destroyed by the Turks in 1543. All the same, it boasts some of Hungary's most prestigious buildings, the most impressive of which is the Basilika, Hungary's largest cathedral. Little remains of the medieval building, with the present neoclassical structure dating from the early 19th century. The Bakócz Chapel is by far the most dominant feature in this sumptuously decorated building. The white marble altar is the work of Florentine craftsmen and was designed by Andreas Ferrucci in 1519. With its many priceless medieval objects, including the 13th-century Hungarian Coronation Cross, the treasury is also the resting place of Cardinal Mindszenty, the cathedral's most famous clergyman. Beside the basilica is the Vár Múzeum (Castle Museum), housing the fascinating remains of the former royal palace.

Don't miss the Keresztény Múzeum (Christian Museum), containing the best collection of medieval religious art in Hungary, and also works by Italian masters Duccio, Lorenzo di Credi and Gionvanni di Paola. Since the Danube is such a dominant feature of the town, there's the Duna Múzeum (Danube Museum) to help you understand its evolution. Although most of the captions are in Hungarian, this doesn't lessen the impact of the exhibition.

🚌 Bus: Frequent service from Budapest's Árpád híd bus station.

🚆 Regular service from Nyugati Railway Station

❓ By car: 66km (41 miles), route 10, then 111

ℹ️ Gran Tours ✉ Széchenyi tér 25, Esztergom ☎ 33 502 001

GÖDÖLLŐ

An easy trip by car or suburban train, this small town is dominated by the great baroque palace begun in 1741 by Empress Maria Theresa's favourite courtier, Count Grassalkovich. It is claimed to be outdone in size only by the Palace of Versailles in France, but visitors come here in numbers less for architectural pomp than for the place's associations with another empress, Franz Joseph's consort Elizabeth. 'Sissi', as she was known, fell in love with all things Hungarian, and was loved in return. The palace has been largely restored after use in communist times as an old people's home; Sissi fans will find much evidence of her presence here, though few of the furnishings and fittings are original. An exception is the completely intact baroque theatre, a real rarity. You can walk in the palace's park, dress up as a Habsburg and have your photo taken, or browse among the range of superior souvenirs in the gift shop. Gödöllő was also attractive to artists, and a century ago a utopian artistic colony was formed here, its members coming from as far away as Paris. The town museum has good examples of their work and nicely evokes their earnest, bearded and sandaled way of life. Gödöllő may be far from the *puszta*, but you can admire spectacular horsemanship at the Lazar Equestrian Park nearby, where the traditional atmosphere of the Hungarian countryside has been carefully re-created.

✉ Royal Palace, Grassalkovich Kastély, 2100 Gödöllő ☎ 28 410 124 🍴 Café (€–€€) 🚆 Frequent HÉV suburban trains from Ors vezér tér (terminus of Metro line 2) to Gödöllő Szabadság tér station

❓ By car: 30km (18.6 miles) M3 motorway

Gödöllő town museum

✉ Szabadság tér 5, 2100 Gödöllő ☎ 28 422 003 🕐 Tue–Sun 10–6 ✋ Inexpensive

Lázár Equestrian Park

✉ Lázár Lovaspark, 2182 Gödöllő-Domonyvölgy ☎ 28 576 510; www.lazarlovaspark.hu. Call to check times of shows 🍴 Dining hall (€–€€)

❓ By car: 5 km (3 miles) east of Gödöllő, route 3

SZENTENDRE

Szentendre lies in a beautiful vale of hills beside the Danube. Founded in the 11th century, it takes its name from the guardian angel of its church, Andras (Endre). In the 14th century it became a royal estate, but 150 years of Turkish occupation followed, at the end of which the town was virtually deserted. It was later settled by rich craftsmen and merchants, but the town again went into decline. But much is still intact, and it's worth starting your visit on Fő tér (Main Square), with its huddled houses and alleyways like Jeno Dumsta utca and Bogdani utca, the main shopping and restaurant area. The Memorial Cross in the middle of the square was erected in thanks for the end of the Black Death by the Privileged Merchants' Company in 1763.

Nearby on Fő körút is the Orthodox Episcopal Church, also known as Beograda. Built between 1756–64, its baroque architecture houses an ornamented and decorated interior. The splendid Margit Kovács Museum is one of the most delightful galleries in Szentendre and houses the works of the famous ceramicist after whom it is named. For superb views of the town, and a pleasant walk as well, take a stroll up to Templom tér, Szentendre's highest point, where a narrow cobbled lane leads up to the square. From here you'll be treated to a cavalcade of russet roof tiles sloping down to the Danube, interrupted by dots of green gardens. No trip to the town of Szentendre would be complete without a visit to the fascinating Szabadadtéri Néprajzi Muzeum (Open-air Museum of the Hungarian Village). Originals of houses, buildings and machines were reassembled here to represent the country's vernacular architecture.

🚉 HÉV train: From Budapest's Batthyány tér station every 10 to 20 minutes
🚌 Bus: From Budapest's Áprád híd station, takes 30 minutes
🚢 From Mar–Oct. Contact Mahart PassNave ☎ 14 844 013;
www.mahartpassnave.hu ❓ By car: 20km (12.4 miles), route 11

VISEGRÁD

Offering magnificent views of the Danube, Visegrád (a Slav name meaning 'lofty fortress') lies on the river's abrupt loop between the Pilis and Börzsöny Hills. The town dates from Roman times when the Danube formed the border of the Roman Empire. After the Mongul invasion, the Hungarian kings built the imposing citadel dominating the hilltop above Solomon's Tower. During the Turkish occupation Visegrád was virtually destroyed, and later the Habsburgs blew up the citadel to prevent its use by Hungarian independence fighters. Now undergoing restoration, the best way to reach it is by the excellent hiking trails, following signposts marked 'Fellegvár', starting from behind the Catholic church.

The other major sight worth looking at in Visegrád is the 14th-century Royal Palace. Largely destroyed by the Habsburgs in 1702, the building has been under excavation since 1934. Highlights here include replicas of the red-marbled Hercules Fountain in the Gothic courtyard and the Lion Fountain.

🚌 Bus: Regular return service from Budapest's Árpád Bridge station.

🚆 Train: Services run to Szob (24 daily) from Budapest-Nyugati station. Get off at Nagymaros-Visegrád and take a ferry across to Visegrád

🚢 Mahart hydrofoil links Budapest and Esztergom via Visegrád; see www.mahartpassnave.hu for times and prices

🚗 By car: 40km (25 miles), route 11

ℹ️ Visegrád Tours, Rév utca 15 ☎ 26 398 160

HOTELS

BUDAI-HEGYEK
Café Picard (€)

This small café built in the 1930s still retains its original art-deco fittings, and serves sandwiches and brochettes alongside warmer dishes like Thai shrimp soup.

✉ Pasaréti tér, Budapest II ☎ 392 7530

ESZTERGOM
Hotel Esztergom (€€)

One of the principal hotels in this fascinating old town, offering all modern facilities for its 36 rooms. Well placed for all the main attractions and sights.

✉ Prímás-sziget, Nagy-Duna sétány ☎ (33) 412 555; www.hotels.hu/esztergom

Ria Pension (€€)

Close to the Basilica, this family-run pension has 15 comfortable rooms and added extras like a fitness room, sauna, internet access and bike rental.

✉ Batthyány Lajos utca 11–13 ☎ (33) 313 115; www.riapension.com

Csülök Csárda (€)

Home-style Hungarian cooking and pork knuckles are the specialties of this pleasant little restaurant next door to Ria Pension.

✉ Batthyány Lajos utca 9 ☎ (33) 412 420

SZENTENDRE
Centrum (€€)

Centrum is located close to the river in a lovingly restored one-storey village house. Its rooms are bright and breezy and come with antique furniture.

✉ Dunakorzó ☎ 302 500; www.hotelcentrum.hu

Ilona (€)

Ilona is suitably central but not in the heart of the action. Its rooms may be a little small, but they're quite cosy and clean and breakfast is served in a peaceful inner courtyard. Locked parking is also available.

✉ Rákóczi Ferenc utca 11 ☎ 313 599

Aranysárkány (€€)
Aranysárkány is a central choice with fine Hungarian and Austrian cuisine.

✉ Alkotmány utca 1/a ☎ (26) 301 479

Promenade (€€)
Closer to the river, this pleasant restaurant has a mix of Hungarian and international dishes, and a large, breezy terrace.

✉ Futó utca 4 ☎ (26) 312 626

VISEGRÁD
Haus Honti (€€)
Close to the centre of Visegrád and the Danube, Honti has modern hotel rooms and simpler (and cheaper) pension rooms. Bicycles are also available for rent.

✉ Fő utca 66 ☎ (26) 398 120

Grill Udvar (€)
Small and basic, Grill Udvar offers a touch of provincial Hungarian cooking and service in the heart of Visegrád village.

✉ Rév utca 6 ☎ No phone

ENTERTAINMENT

BUDAI-HEGYEK
Gyermekvasút (Children's Railway)
See page 63.

Libegő (Chairlift)
See page 63.

Index

Street index

Acknowledgements

The Automobile Association wishes to thank the following photographers, companies and picture libraries for their assistance in the preparation of this book.

Abbreviations for the picture credits are as follows – (t) top; (b) bottom; (l) left; (r) right; (c) centre; (AA) AA World Travel Library.

4l Parliament over the Danube, AA/G Wrona; **4c** Tram 2, AA/J Smith; **4r** View from Castle Hill, AA/J Smith; **5l** Rudas Baths and Gellert Hill, AA/J Smith; **5c** Szechenyi Chain Bridge, AA/J Smith; **5r** Cathedral, Esztergom, AA/K Paterson; **6/7** Parliament over the Danube, AA/G Wrona; **8/9** Gresham Palace, AA/P Wilson; **10/11t** Basilica, Eger, AA/P Wilson; **10c** Korzo promenade, AA/J Smith; **10b** Hilton Hotel Lobby, AA/P Wilson; **10/11b** View of the Danube, AA/P Wilson; **11** Eugene of Savoy Statue, AA/J Smith; **12c** Jokai bean soup, Karolyi restaurant, AA/J Smith; **12b** Paprika, AA/J Smith; **12/13** The Central Hotel, Budapest, AA/J Smith; **13t** Nokedli at Karolyi Restaurant, AA/J Smith; **13b** Butcher's Staff, Nagycsarnok, AA/J Smith; **14** Café of Vaci Utca, **14/15** Tokaji Wine, AA/J Smith; **16/17** Shops on Vaci Utca, AA/J Smith; **16b** Fisherman's Bastion, AA/J Smith; **17c** Szechenyi Chain Bridge and Buda Castle Palace at night, AA/J Smith; **17b** Vorosmarty ter, drinkers, AA/J Smith; **18** Margaret Island, Water Tower, AA/J Smith; **19t** Rudas Baths, AA/K Paterson; **19b** Budapest Royal Palace, AA/K Paterson; **20/21** Tram 2, AA/J Smith; **25** Folk Music performance, AA/K Paterson; **27** Cogwheels Railway Terminus, AA/J Smith; **34/35** View from Castle Hill, AA/J Smith; **36** Hungarian National Gallery, AA/K Paterson; **36/37** Buda Castle Palace, AA/J Smith; **38/39** Gellert Hill, view over the Danube, AA/K Paterson; **39** Gellert Hill and the Liberation Monument, AA/J Smith; **40/41** Statue, Fisherman's Bastion, AA/P Wilson; **41** Statue, Fisherman's Bastion, AA/J Smith; **42/43** State Opera House, AA/J Smith; **43** Old Fashioned State Opera sign, AA/J Smith; **44** Margaret Island Gardens, AA/J Smith; **45** View from Fisherman's Bastion over Margaret Island, AA/J Smith; **46** Matthias Church and Fisherman's Bastion, AA/J Smith; **47** Matthais Church, AA/J Smith; **48/49** Parliament and the Chain

Every effort has been made to trace the copyright holders, and we apologise in advance for any unintentional omissions or errors. We would be pleased to apply any corrections in any following edition of this publication.

Sight locator index

Dear Reader

Your comments, opinions and recommendations are very important to us. Please help us to improve our travel guides by taking a few minutes to complete this simple questionnaire.

You do not need a stamp (unless posted outside the UK). If you do not want to cut this page from your guide, then photocopy it or write your answers on a plain sheet of paper.

Send to: **The Editor, AA World Travel Guides,**
FREEPOST SCE 4598, Basingstoke RG21 4GY.

Your recommendations...

We always encourage readers' recommendations for restaurants, nightlife or shopping – if your recommendation is used in the next edition of the guide, we will send you a **FREE AA Guide** of your choice from this series. Please state below the establishment name, location and your reasons for recommending it.

_____
_____
_____
_____
_____
_____

Please send me **AA Guide** _____

About this guide...

Which title did you buy?

AA _____

Where did you buy it?_____

When? m̲ m̲ / y̲ y̲

Why did you choose this guide? _____
_____
_____
_____
_____

Did this guide meet your expectations?

Exceeded ☐   Met all ☐   Met most ☐   Fell below ☐

Were there any aspects of this guide that you particularly liked? _____
_____
_____
_____

continued on next page...

Is there anything we could have done better? _____
_____
_____
_____

About you...
Name (*Mr/Mrs/Ms*) _____
Address _____
_____
_____ Postcode _____

Daytime tel nos _____
Email _____

Please only give us your mobile phone number or email if you wish to hear from us about other products and services from the AA and partners by text or mms, or email.

Which age group are you in?
Under 25 ☐   25–34 ☐   35–44 ☐   45–54 ☐   55–64 ☐   65+ ☐

How many trips do you make a year?
Less than one ☐   One ☐   Two ☐   Three or more ☐

Are you an AA member? Yes ☐   No ☐

About your trip...
When did you book? m m / y y   When did you travel? m m / y y

How long did you stay? _____

Was it for business or leisure? _____

Did you buy any other travel guides for your trip? _____

If yes, which ones? _____
_____
_____

Thank you for taking the time to complete this questionnaire. Please send it to us as soon as possible, and remember, you do not need a stamp (*unless posted outside the UK*).

| **AA** Travel Insurance call 0800 072 4168 or visit www.theAA.com |